I0531806

Ordering Information:
Contact author at teamvelasquez@hotmail.com or order online

Gratitude Saved Me/ Carolina Ayala-Velasquez. —1st ed.
ISBN 979-8-9855006-1-5

GRATITUDE SAVED ME

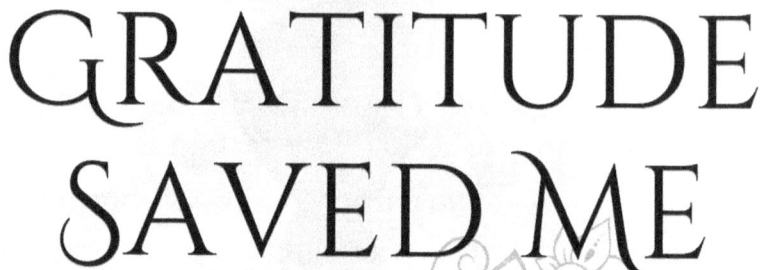

JOURNAL
PROMPTS AND
REFLECTIONS

Carolina Ayala-
Velasquez

A life I once only dreamed of.

I believe there is something very powerful about showing up as you are; being unpolished, unrehearsed and real. No one can tell your story like you can. We all have stories to tell. I believe honesty creates opportunity for release and healing; and it also creates the space to make genuine connections. Thank you for being a part of making my dream a reality by supporting me on this author journey. I am not just living a childhood dream or a life-long dream. I am living many dream come trues every time I get to create a book and reach someone new. I will continue to share my whole self, in hopes to inspire others to do the same. Sharing gratitude in this way, with the world- is helping me live in my purpose.

Dedicated to someone special.

To my younger self, my future self, and my present self.

Dedicated to my children, family, friends and even those I don't yet know or may never know.

What is a gratitude journal?

What would make mine different?

What does it mean?

How do you find daily gratitude?

What can gratitude do for you?

What can gratitude give to you and your life?

Can I help you find gratitude?

Can I help you in finding something to be thankful for?

Not help you pretend your anger, pain, challenge, guilt, grief, and those uncomfortable feelings don't exist.

Not help you fake it till you make it. But, truly help you find gratitude- especially in moments when it feels impossible.

I believe in feeling your feelings, and then finding more.
A lesson, a gift, an answered prayer or a thank you.

What makes my journal different is the people I will reach, because I am me. What makes my journal different is my journey and stories shared.

Have you ever been told "Just be thankful for what you have?" I know I have and it doesn't always resonate because sometimes we have moments that aren't positive or full of gratitude. Sometimes we have to feel the hard stuff first.
Start with where you are. I am grateful for feeling my feelings. I am thankful for the choices to change my direction. I am thankful I have people who can see the bright side. Maybe their bright-side isn't mine, and that's ok that it isn't my truth. I am thankful for my truth and my journey, even in the hard times. Maybe you start with "I am being thankful because I am being told to be." But eventually you make it matter to you.

What matters to you?
You start somewhere. It is a choice to choose to be grateful. Especially in the hard times.
With enough practice, gratitude has become easier for me. I can now think of several positives to every negative thought/feeling and I am sure in the past it wasn't always this easy. I am sure in the past it was hard to even think of one positive during a negative time. It truly has become second nature to me, even first.

This journal is not because it is easy to find gratitude. I am not perfect at this choice and lifestyle, but I have built up the practice my whole life. It doesn't mean I don't ever get upset, or complain, or even get frustrated with the fact that I am positive and grateful. Challenging times happen, for me and all of us. Having the skill to see, and choose gratitude helps ease my mind and my body.
Gratitude helps me find peace.

Sometimes complaining, helps me get it "out" and then find my way to the gratitude. To look for the opposites of all of my troubles. I believe we need to feel our feelings, and somehow, we can move from that place of realness. Sometimes what goes wrong, helps me see what's going right. It is ok to complain, to be upset, to feel other emotions other than thankfulness and happiness and hope. We are human.

It's a thin line between two very different thoughts/feelings and actions. You can make space for both.

Reframing serves me well.
Thankfulness is not a one-time thing or a holiday thing. It isn't just something we dig into during funerals or celebrations.
(It doesn't have to be.)
It is an everyday thing. It is a practice. A choice. That you have to intentionally choose, over and over again.

Language matters. You can take control of your narrative.

"It could be better." "It could be worse." What if it isn't about better or worse. What if good and bad aren't about being good or bad but it's all neutral and natural.

Choosing to think differently. Choosing to practice a new thought. Choosing to entertain something else. We are always one thought away from a different choice. Always one choice away from a different result.

You wanna change your life? You gotta change your mind.

Gratitude

Prompts

Why am I not Grateful?

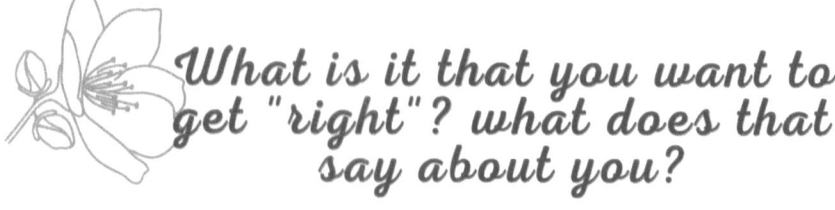

What is it that you want to get "right"? what does that say about you?

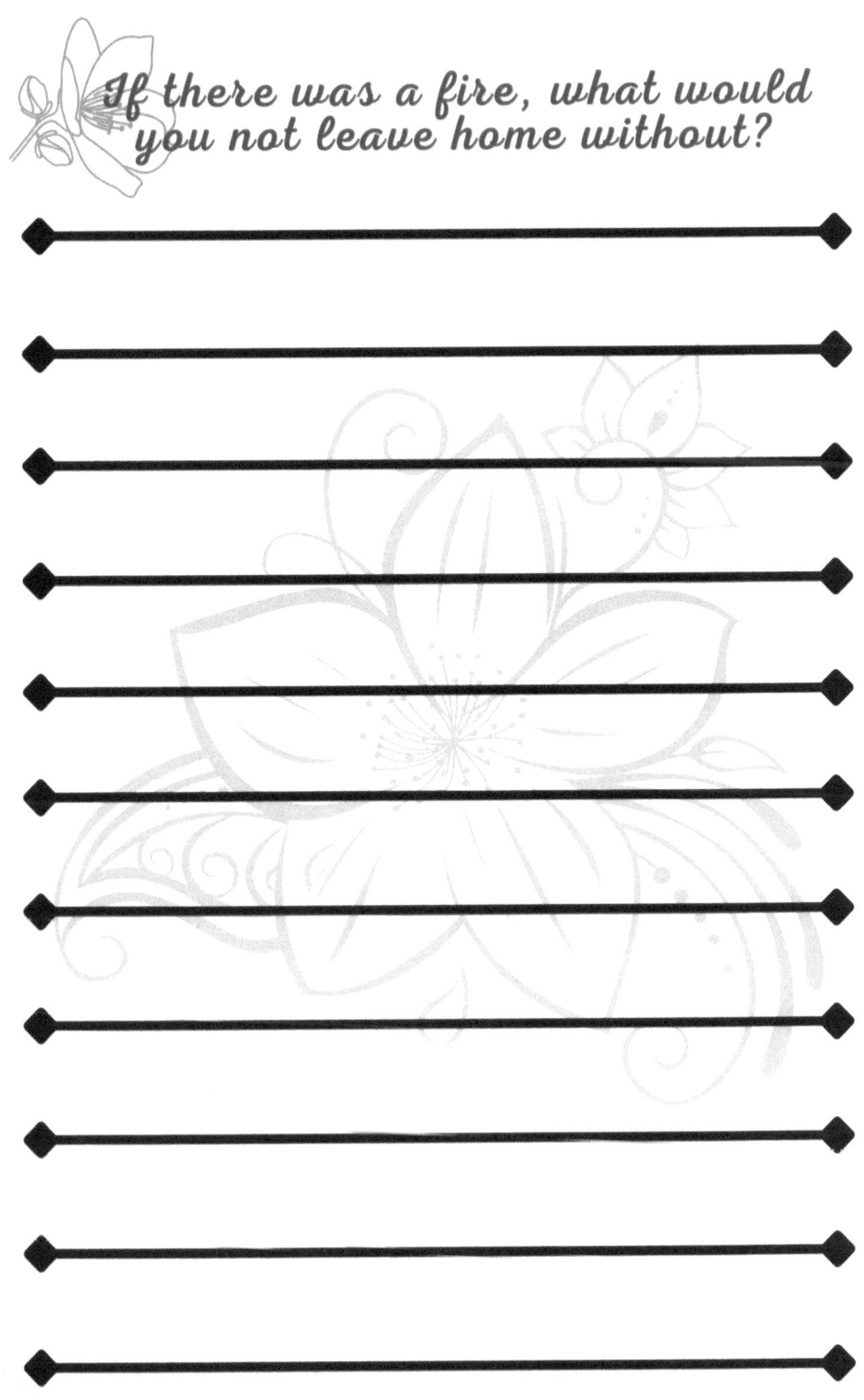

If there was a fire, what would you not leave home without?

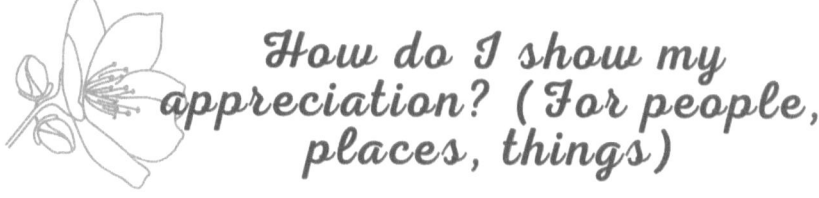

How do I show my appreciation? (For people, places, things)

Imagine your 100th birthday. What do people appreciate about you/thank you for?

_____

_____

_____

_____

_____

_____

_____

_____

_____

_____

In what ways do I like to be appreciated?

When do I feel that people don't appreciate me?

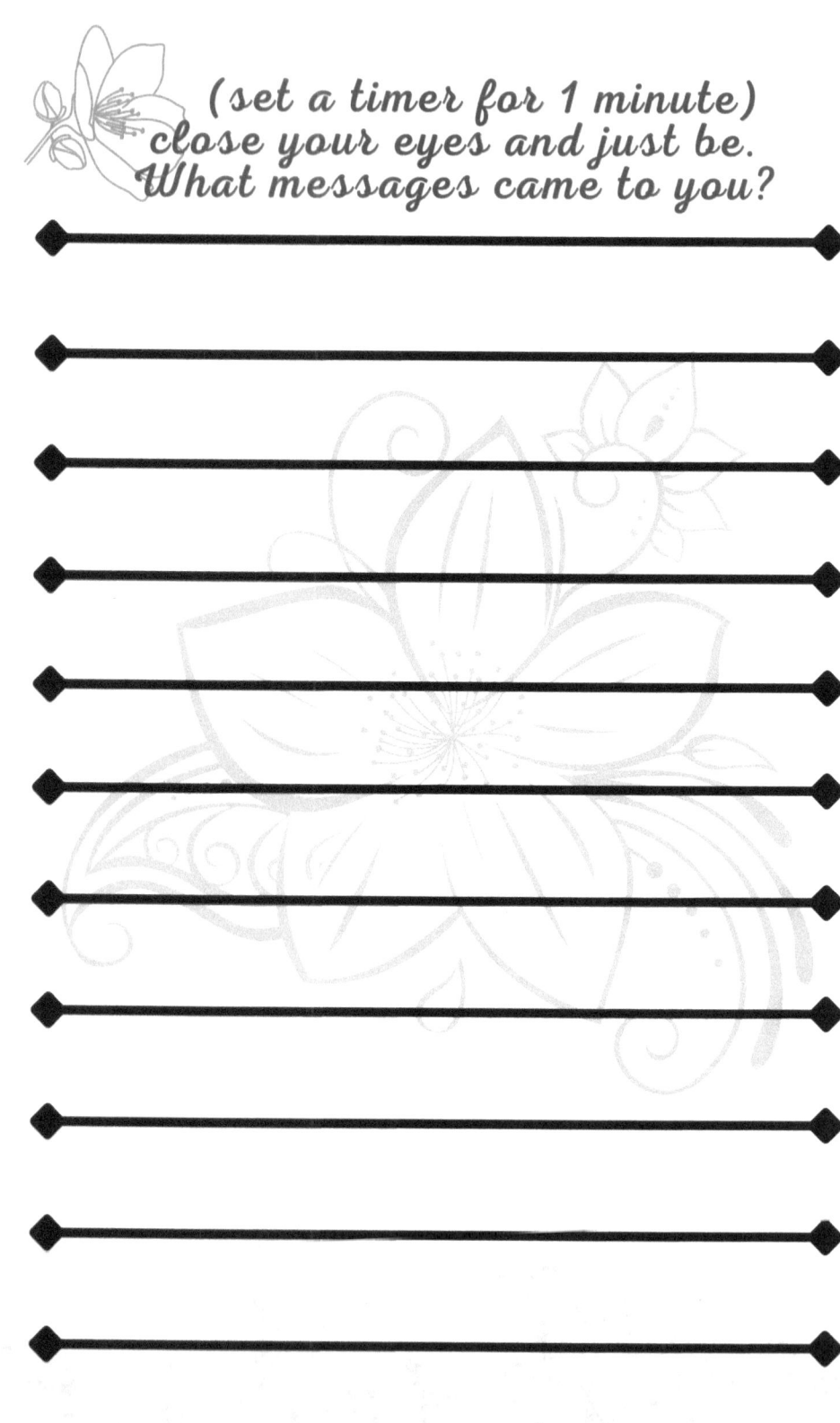

(set a timer for 1 minute)
close your eyes and just be.
What messages came to you?

For as long as I could remember I had lived a very anxious life.

As a child, I was always worried about what the last picture with loved ones would be or if I would wake up the next day.

I would stay awake until after midnight to assure myself that I made it to the next day. My family was in and out of jail so I was programmed to believe that I would have to go without them.

When I became a parent, I was very happy and very anxious. I wanted to be a good role model.

I wanted to make the right choices, even if I didn't know what they were.

When any of my children would sneeze or cough or anything- I would freak out and my brain would always think the worst first of any situation.

As I got older, I knew I had anxiety and thought I couldn't change it.
That it was just who I was. And not only did I have anxiety, but I had severe anxiety.

I couldn't leave the house without unplugging everything and turning everything off and locking everything up, and then still wondering if I did after I had left.

It wasn't until the year before the pandemic that I was shaken out of my comfort zone. We had to move from the home/city/schools that we had been with for more than half of my life and all of my kid's life at the time.

The job I had dreamed of and been a part of for so long, shut down at this same time. I held gratitude for it all. For the memories, opportunities, and new beginnings.

But I didn't know then, how depressed I was and going to be until much later.

These transitions eventually lead me to feel faint, have anxiety/panic attacks, and get myself counseling (which I still am involved with.) It took that year to process so much. I gave myself time to be real, time to break down, time to complain, time to see all the good, and time to feel good about the good.

At the beginning of 2020, we were asked if we wanted to move back into our "old house." Our lease would be up in March and we had to sit with the idea but my heart knew that's what I had been wanting and manifesting. In March of 2020, we moved back by the first of that month.

I finally felt "home." I did have to grieve this move as well. I had to grieve the loss of great schools and a huge space. All of the happiness for what was happening was way bigger than any feeling of loss. I had dreamed of the life I would live if we ever moved back.

I had made promises to myself, that I knew what I wanted and would not let anything stop me this time from living that life and being this better version of myself I was becoming.
So, when the pandemic found its way not long after we moved in, when places were empty, when we were in music class at the library and it got shut down due to what was happening, I was sad.

I was sad that what I had come back for was all slipping from my grasp. I was determined though. To continue to get out, take walks, breathe fresh air, and enjoy this neighborhood and life.

As lockdowns and shelters in place and curfews came to be I embraced it all. I embraced the good and I stuck to my heart to live a life that brought me peace and happiness.

My past self would not have been able to handle all that was going on or wrong. I would have been freaking out over this illness and changes and unknowns. My past self would have been very obedient, scared, and anxious.
Instead, I had to go with the ever-changing changes, know the facts, listen to my heart and intuition and create the life I wanted.
I continued on my healing journey, embracing free groups and investing in myself to be in spaces of coaching and growing.

The pandemic came with deaths, sickness, loss of relationships, changes in relationships, fear, and having to stand in our truths. It came with judgment, loss, and transformation. For me it was a time to continue to dream, to continue doing new things in hopes of different results.

This time for me was a time of building my faith, community, and connections and giving my intentions the attention, they deserved to become reality.

I had been building my gratitude muscle my whole life. I had been practicing new ways of thinking and working on myself (my whole life) but so much the year leading up to the pandemic. I am not saying any of this time has been easy for me, but I can also see how some may not have such ease during such a challenging time. I am sharing some of my stories to help fill in some pieces of my journey.

I am grateful for dealing with my feelings and transitions. I am grateful for allowing the time. I am grateful for changes pushing us out of our comfort zones, for new experiences, for change and growth. I am grateful for the opportunities we have had.

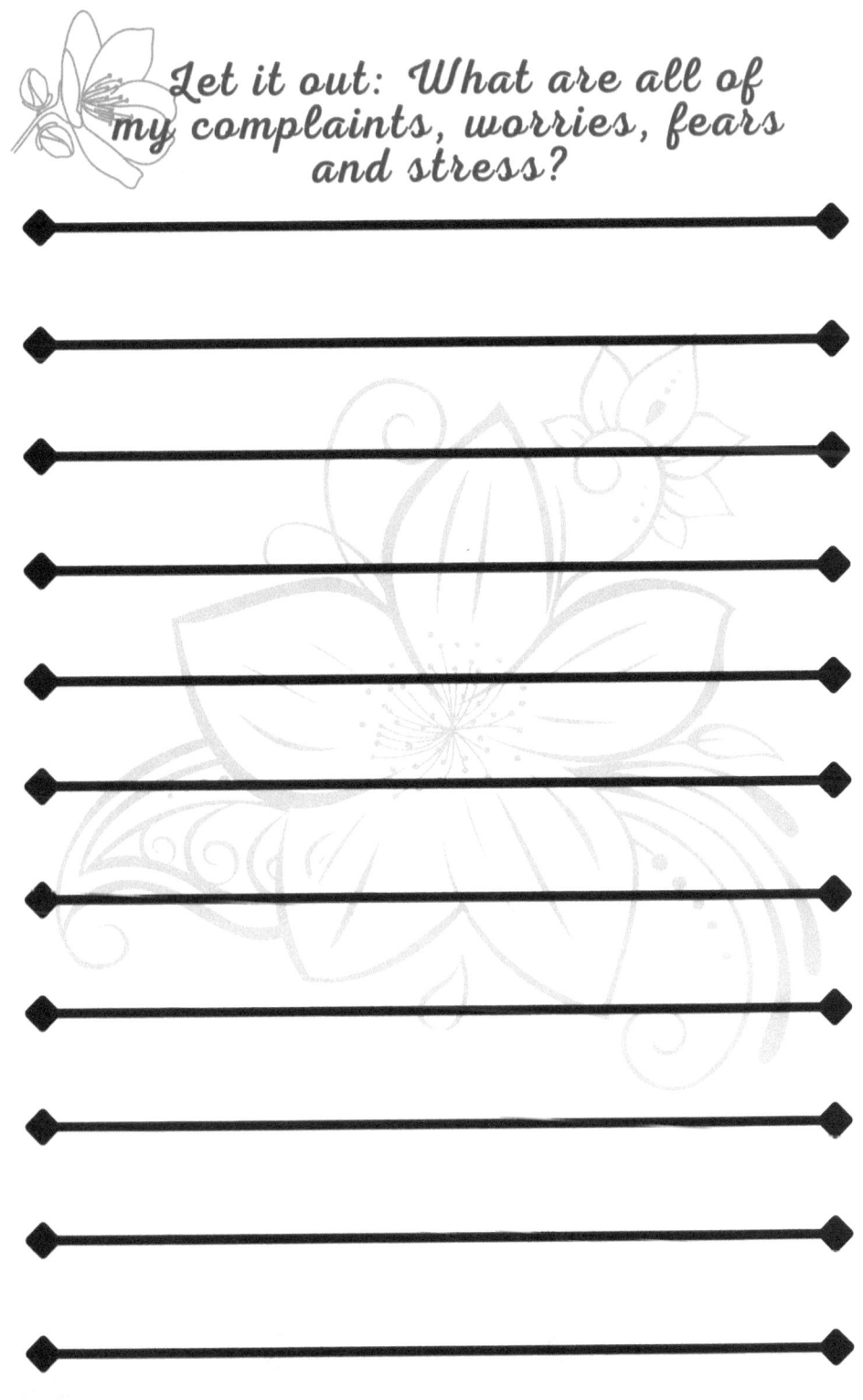

Let it out: What are all of my complaints, worries, fears and stress?

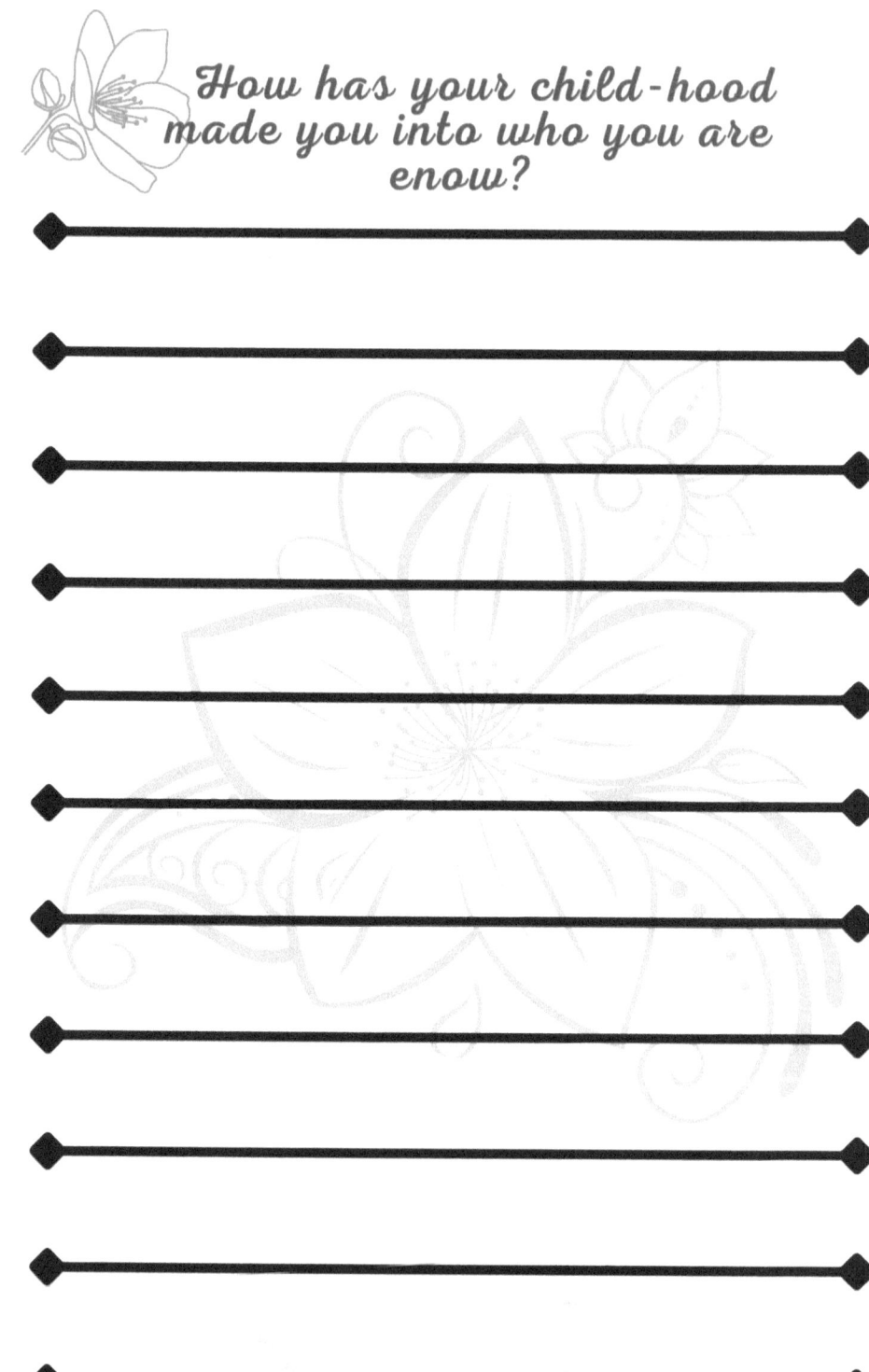

How has your child-hood
made you into who you are
enow?

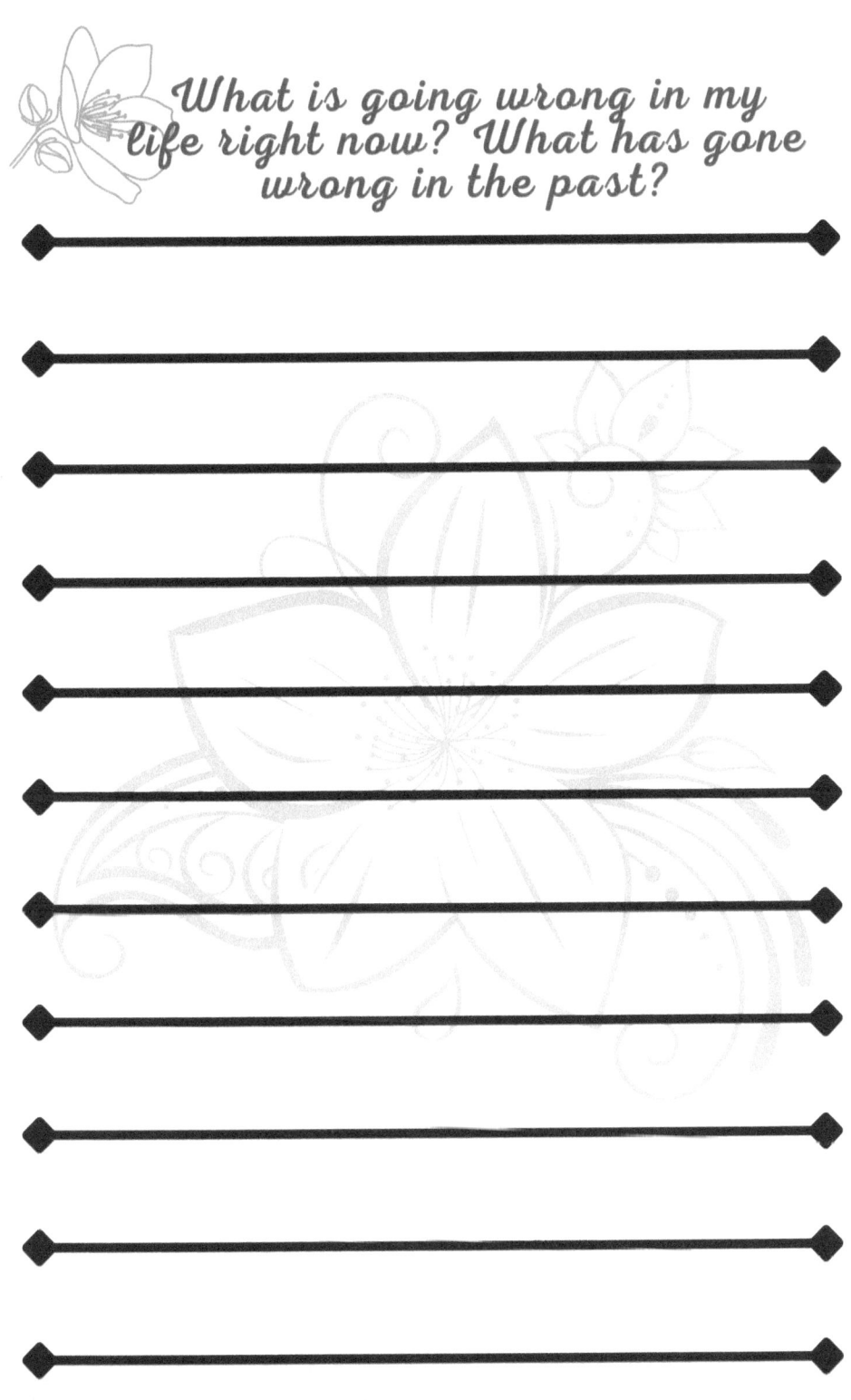

What is going wrong in my life right now? What has gone wrong in the past?

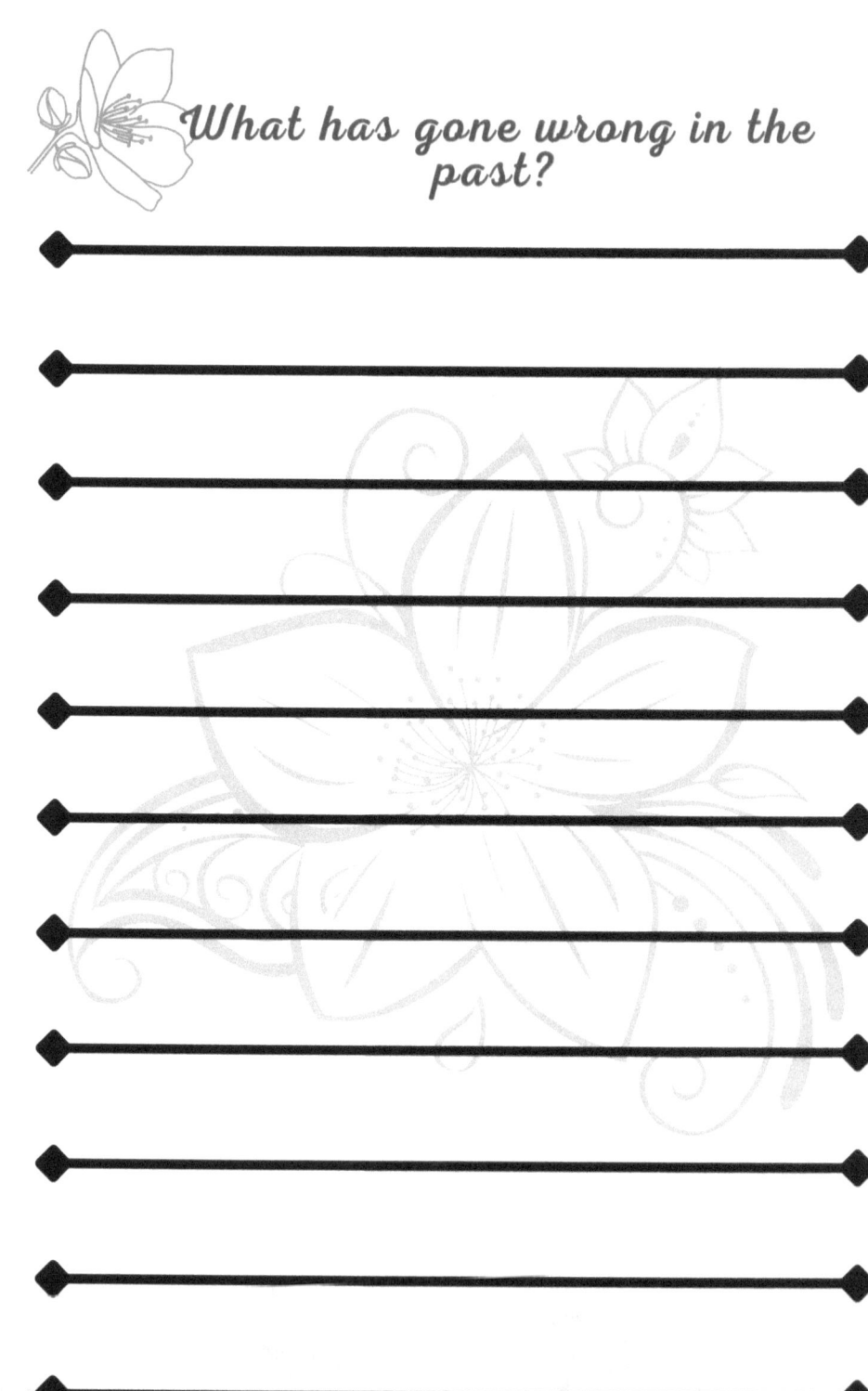

What has gone wrong in the past?

Have you said "thank you" to anyone recently? Or in the past? Maybe you were raised to say thank you, maybe it's a habit, maybe it's intentional. (I believe no matter how you practice or know gratitude; it serves a purpose.)

Can you remember what you said thank you for, and why you were/are thankful?
I feel like this is another way for you to understand gratitude and what it means to you in your life.

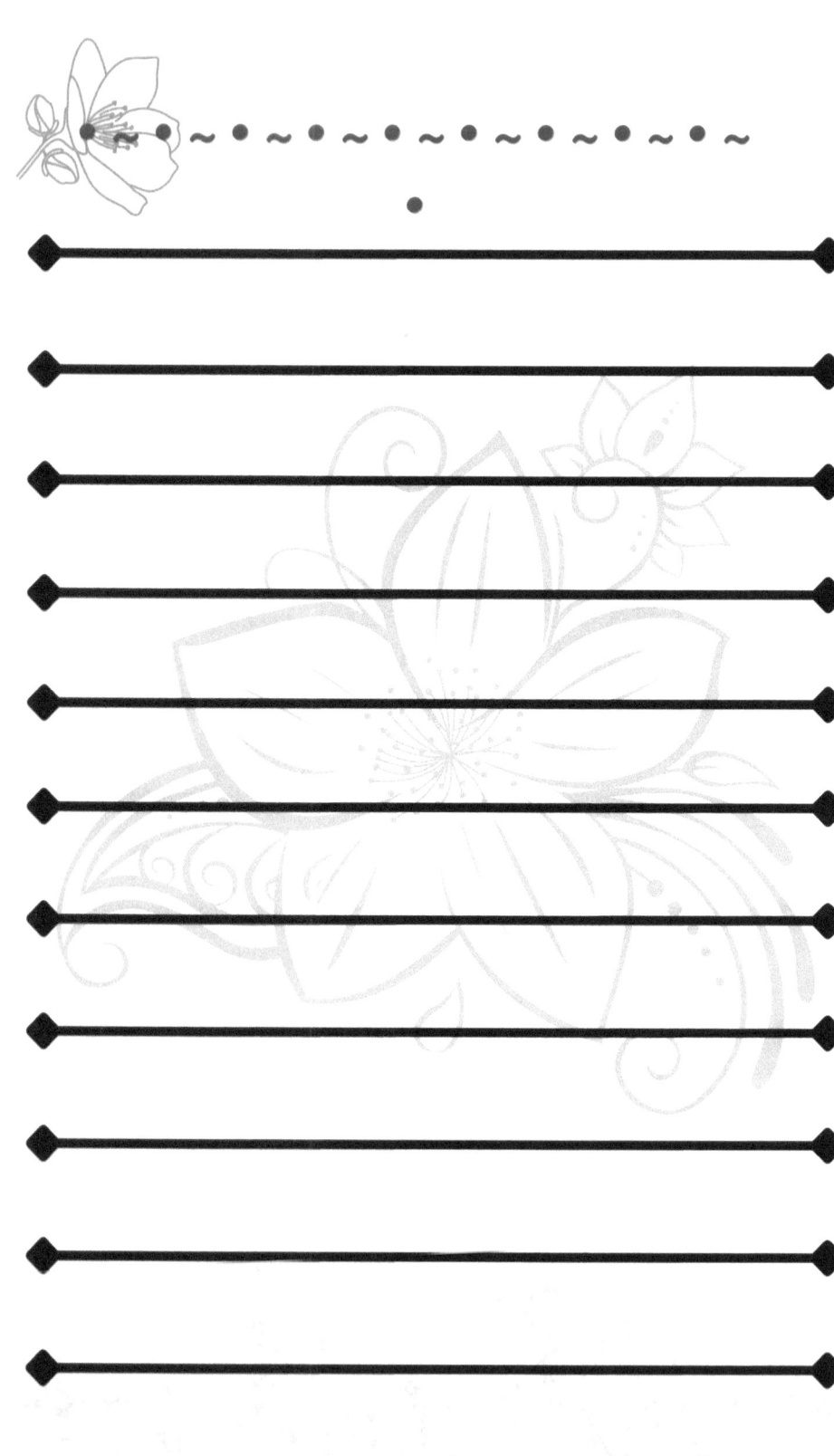

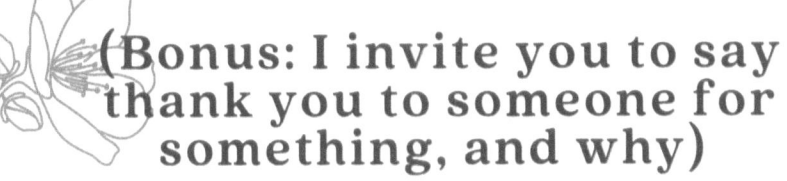

(Bonus: I invite you to say
thank you to someone for
something, and why)

Here is some space to
reflect on that experience,
whether you are choosing to
participate or not.

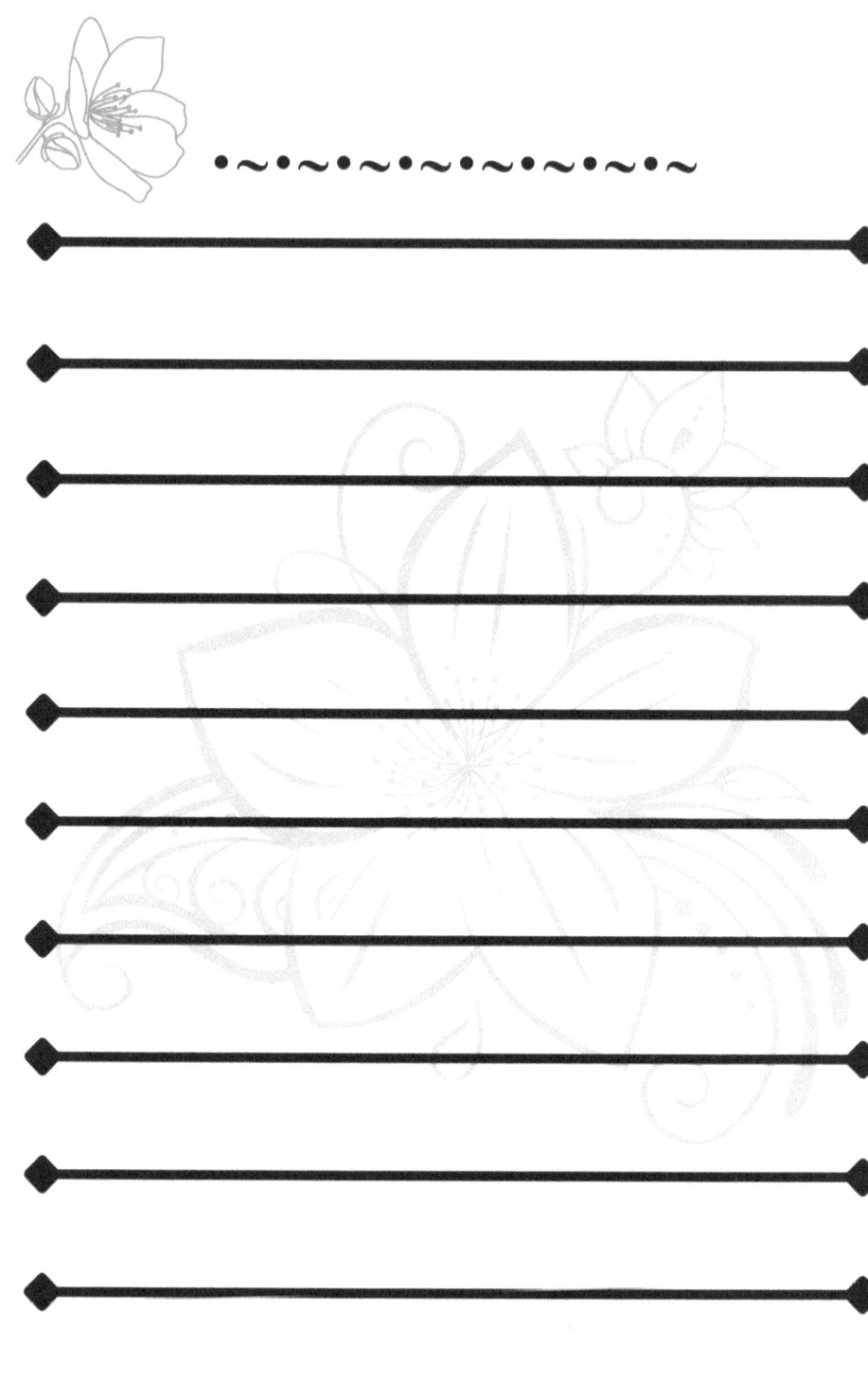

It's been a rough day mentally.
So, when I was asked what I am grateful for today, what came to mind was that I am thankful and I am trying to be thankful for this pain because, although it hurts so bad

It has made me ask myself these questions:
What can help me feel better? what tools do I have? what support can I lean into? what is worth pushing through and what can wait?
Thank you pain. For reminding me of what I want to feel like and what I don't want to feel like, what's important to me, and what I can wait for.

Thank you for helping me with patience and showing me new perspectives.
Thank you for all the self-care you pushed me to seek.
Thank you for reminding me of how far I've come and how I'm still healing.
Thank you for today.
Respectfully I am ready for you to go.

I am thankful still, thankful anyways, thankful always.

Even with the painful physical pain today.
I am still thankful.

***********6/24/21*************

Today I woke up in pain but I decided that I wouldn't let it steal my day.

********7/15/21*********

Do you feel any pain right now? Can you thank your pain for something?

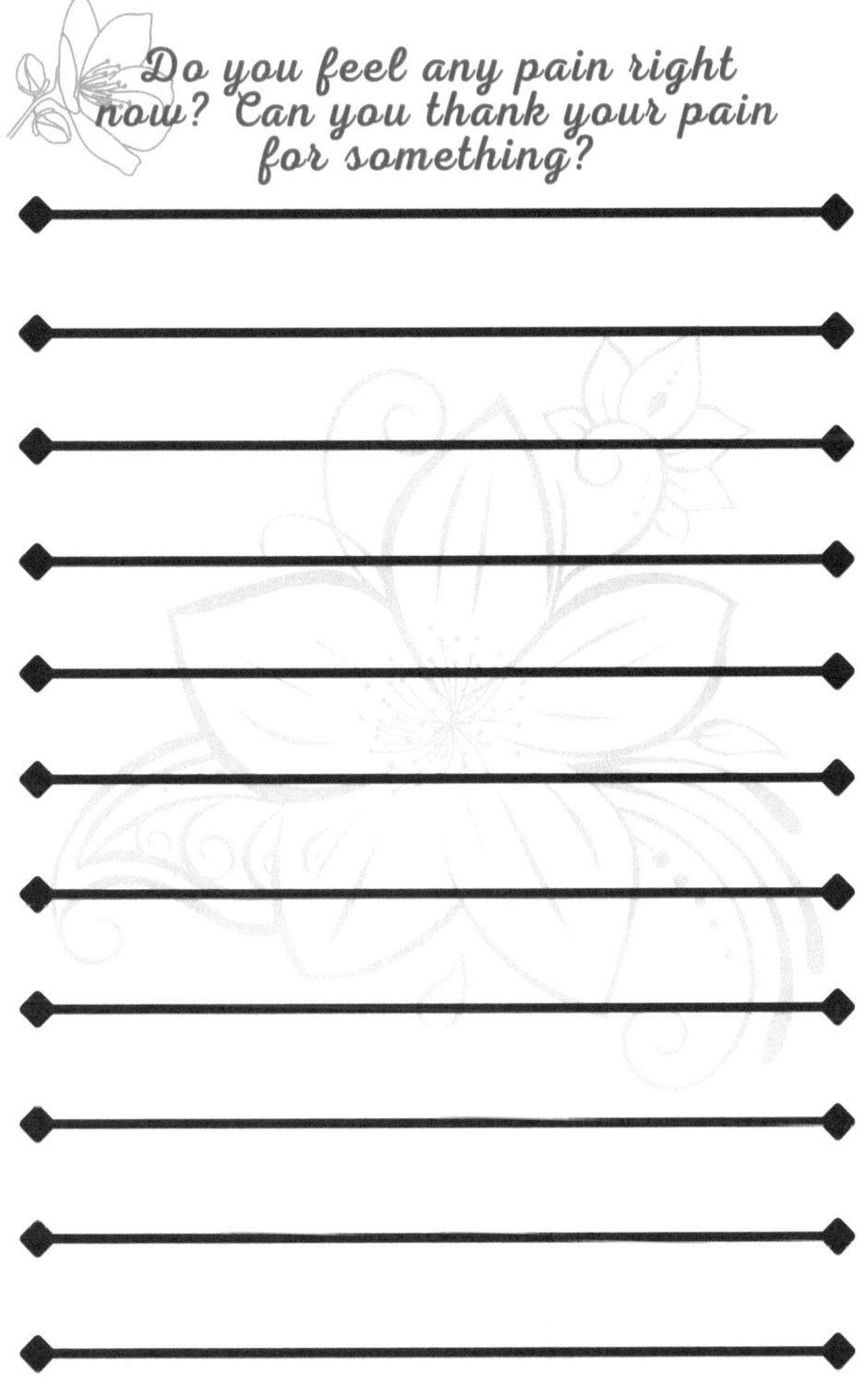

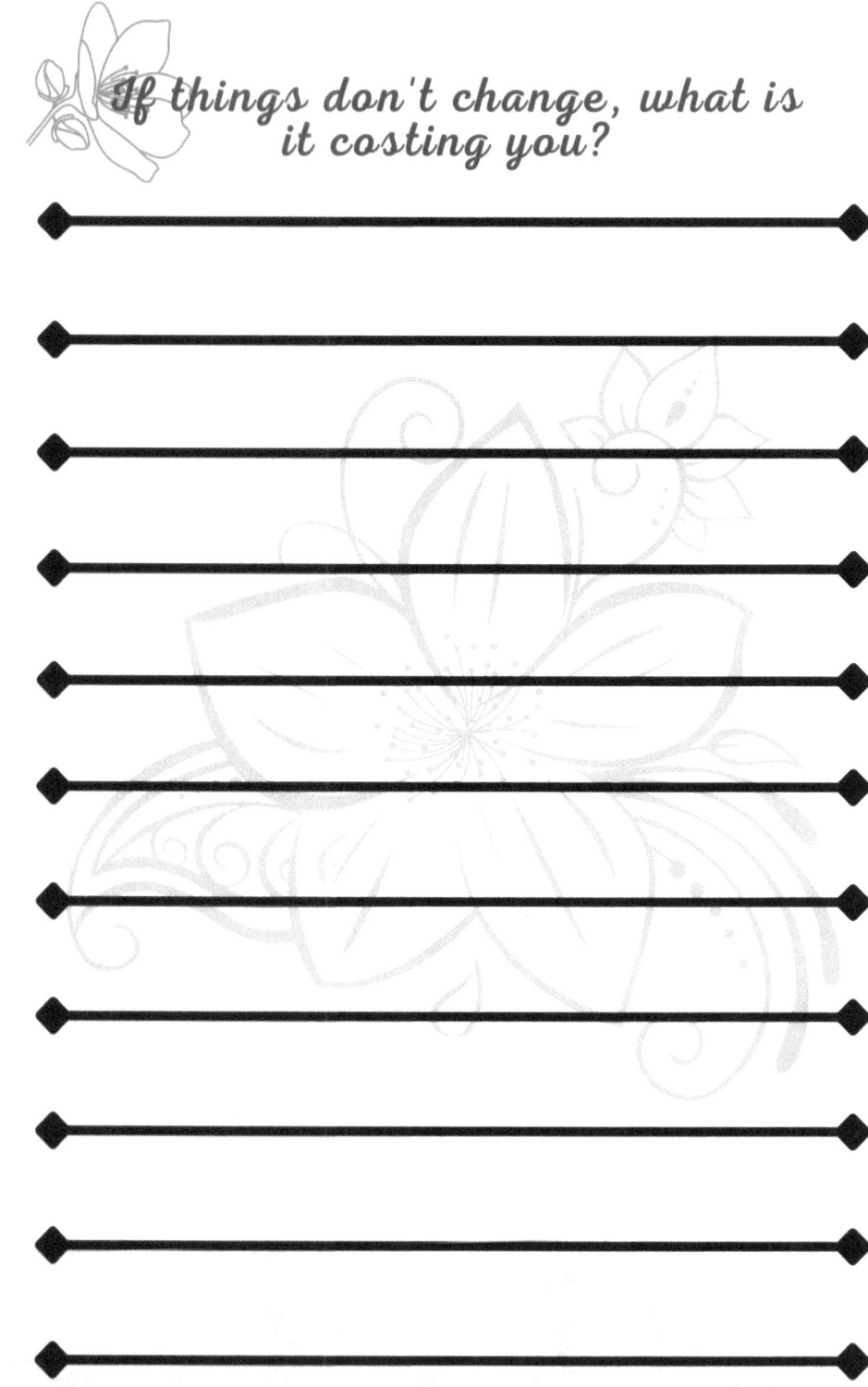

If things don't change, what is it costing you?

Throwing away the "Shoulds" the "Shouldnt's" and thriving anyways.

So much of today was letting go of my shoulds and shouldn't.
This day has been filled with what will serve me today.
More like "at this moment," I can say that I am so thankful I lived in the moments and let life flow.

----6/3/21----
Do I have anything I "should" be doing today? Write them down.

Look at your list, what if you press "pause" or "not at all" on some of those?

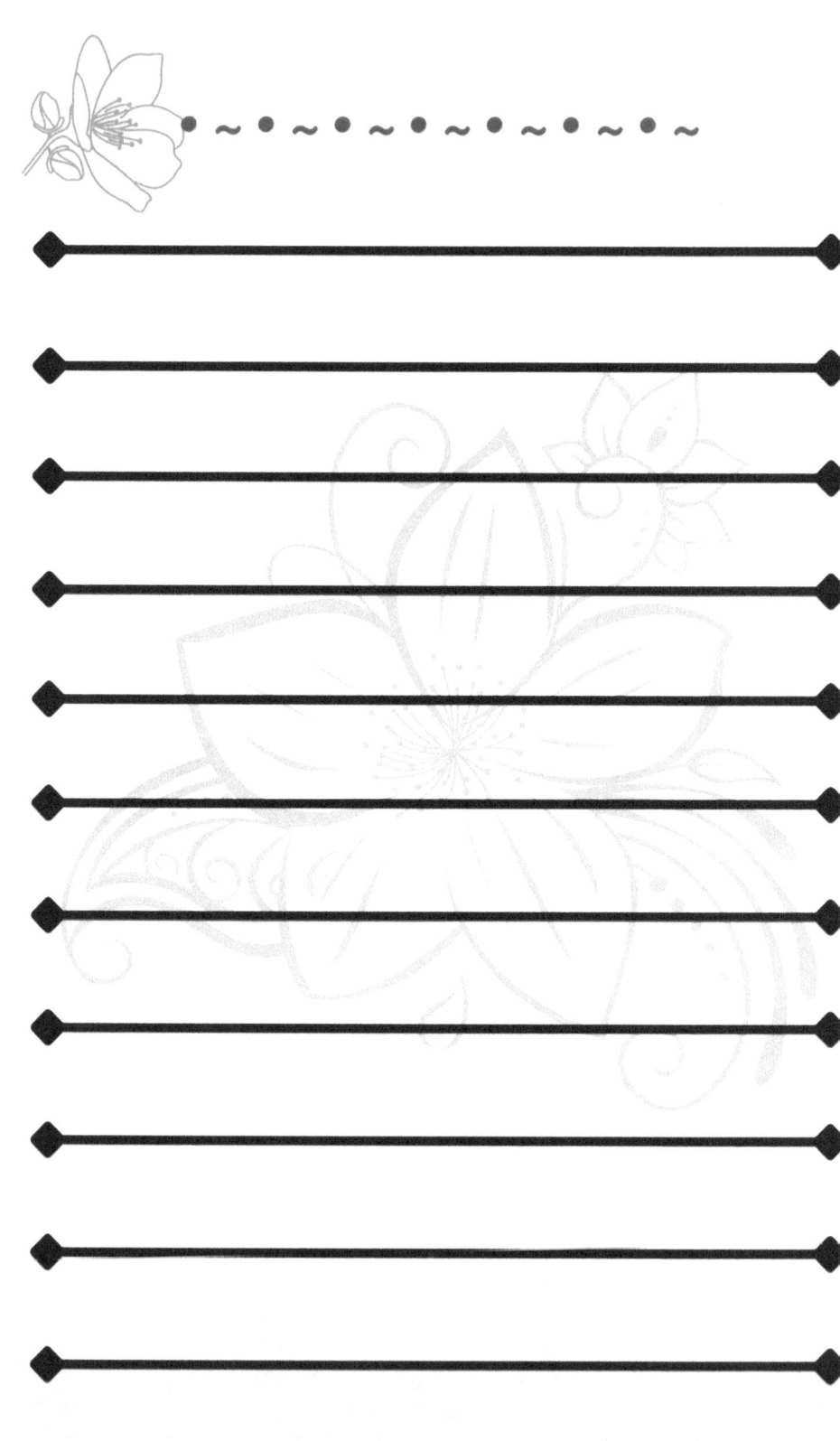

Try thank you instead...
*Thank you ants, I was ignoring that mess on the floor but you helped me get to it.

*Thank you mom, for spilling the watermelon, this spill made me use my steam mop for the second time because I avoided using it again.
"The floor isn't dirty enough" but it was!

*Thank you, friend. you felt like you were "running behind" and worried about changing plan times on me. However, it allowed the kids and I to get into extra walking, extra talking, and extra eating time.
It's crazy, what you can get done when you think you "don't have the time" and you realize how much time you have within each minute.
*Thank you question I finally decided to ask. I didn't get an answer but I got so much more.

Thank you my courage, for saying what is in my mind, for saying what is in my heart, leading to me feeling my dad's spirit alive, seeing his smile, and sharing it.

What a powerful moment. I really needed it, and maybe she too...

*I feel like I've washed those seat covers so many times... Thank you for keeping our chairs and couches clean. Woah, like- for real. Thank you

Can you find a way to reframe your stressful thoughts/situations? Perhaps just once today?
7/12/21
What helps you find clarity when you can't see straight? (For example, try the method I mentioned.
Thank you because_____)

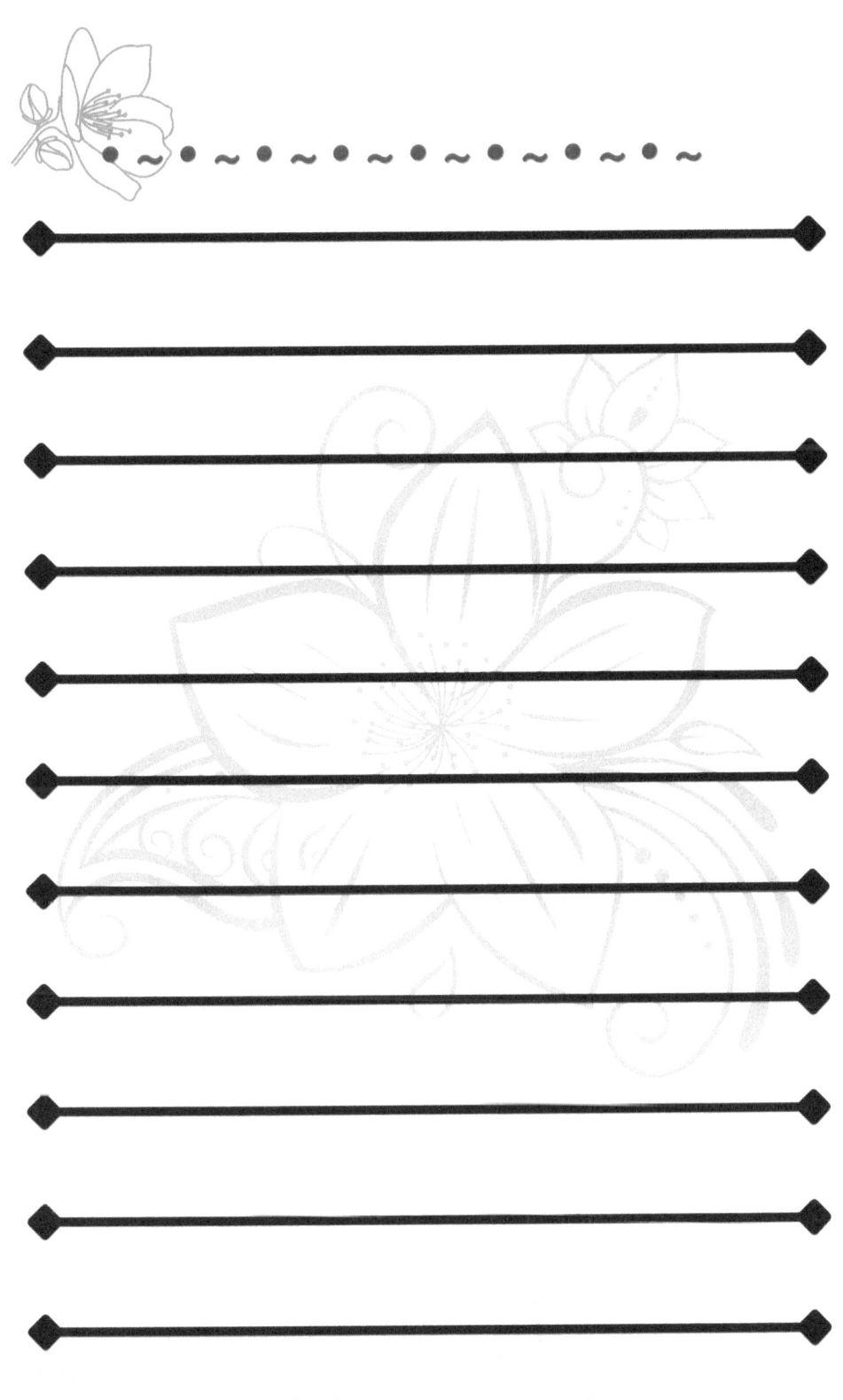

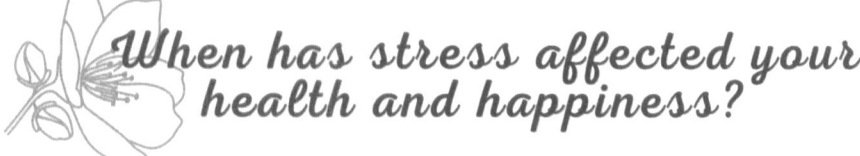

When has stress affected your health and happiness?

We always have a choice.
What thought will you choose
today? What action will you
take? to bring in more joy.

I have been bullied for being too
positive.
I was told that sometimes others think I
am trying to be perfect or trying to
paint a false picture.

I told them and myself that their
thoughts and reflections are theirs to
deal with because I can't control how
others think or feel.
I can only control my actions.

I choose to live a life filled with
gratitude.
Sometimes this can mean that other
people see it as a lifestyle that they don't
agree with or understand.
I will say, it did get to me at some point
in life.
Then, there were two people who I
thought were my friends but they
started picking fights with me.

They even tried to turn others against me because they felt I was "too good" or was trying to be perfect. And that me saying I was living in "goodness" put other people in a bad light.

That hurt me. I felt hurt because I never wanted to hurt anyone.
I never wanted to be the cause of someone's pain.
I remember that I took time to reflect on myself, trying to see what exactly they were seeing. I was trying to figure out if their words held truth.
I was trying to find faults in my gratitude and positivity. Was I not being realistic with myself and others? Was my hope too hopeful?
Was I leading by a false example?

Many years later, I realized what I had done. I realized that their thoughts were from them not me.

One of them came to me later, and said he felt bullied by the other person to "team up against me."
He said they were jealous of the kind of life that I was living and the attitude I had. He shared how much he respects me for who I was then and how he was thankful that I never changed.

But I did change, he just wasn't aware of it.

I started questioning myself. About how I was worried about them. I never took the time to tell him the impact it made.
I accepted his apology and now, we have a rebuilt phase of our relationship, and life kept moving on.

Can you find gratitude in a time you were able to forgive someone?
Who did you forgive and why?

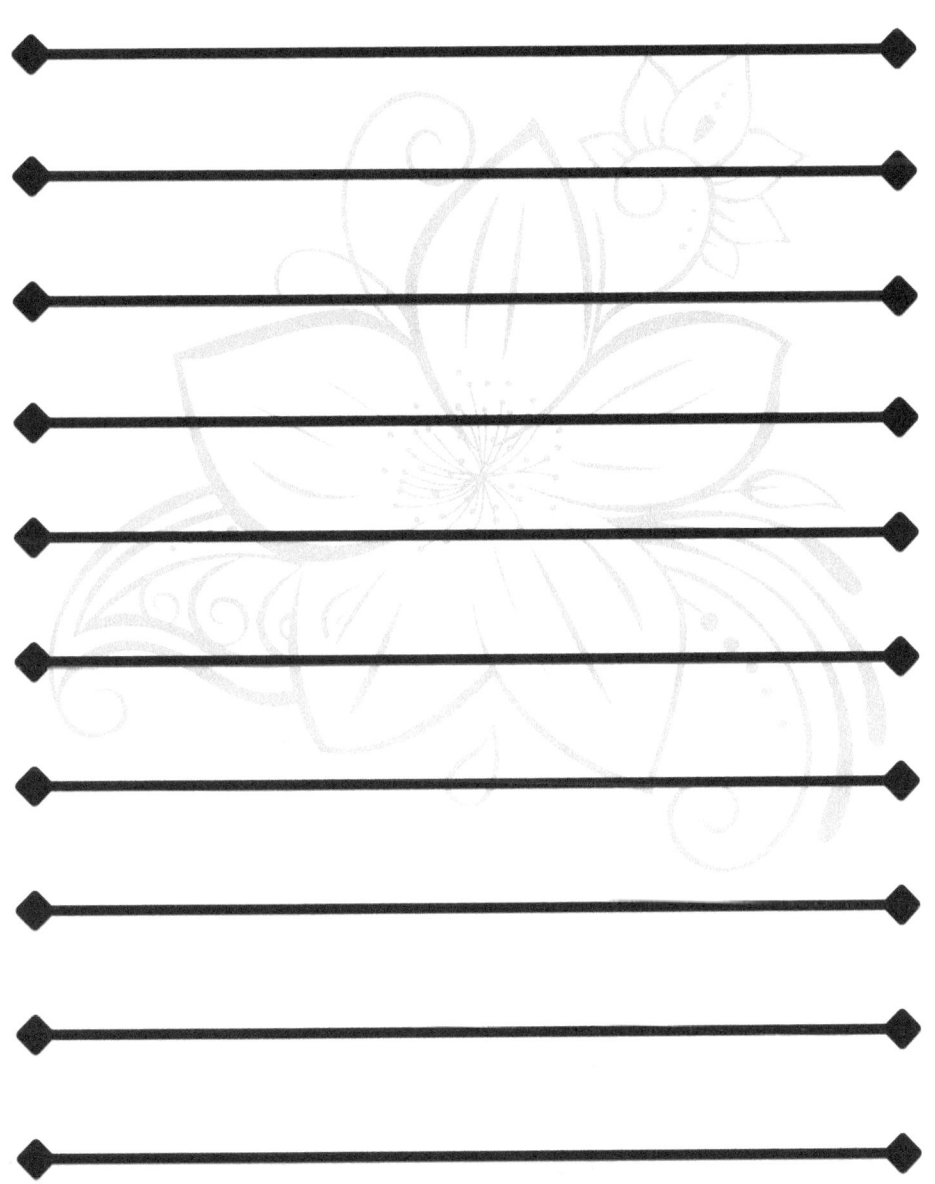

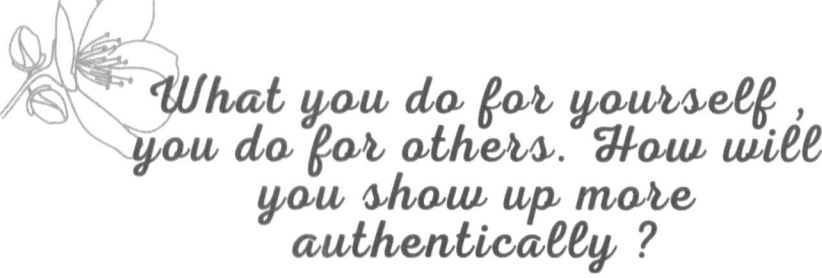

What you do for yourself, you do for others. How will you show up more authentically?

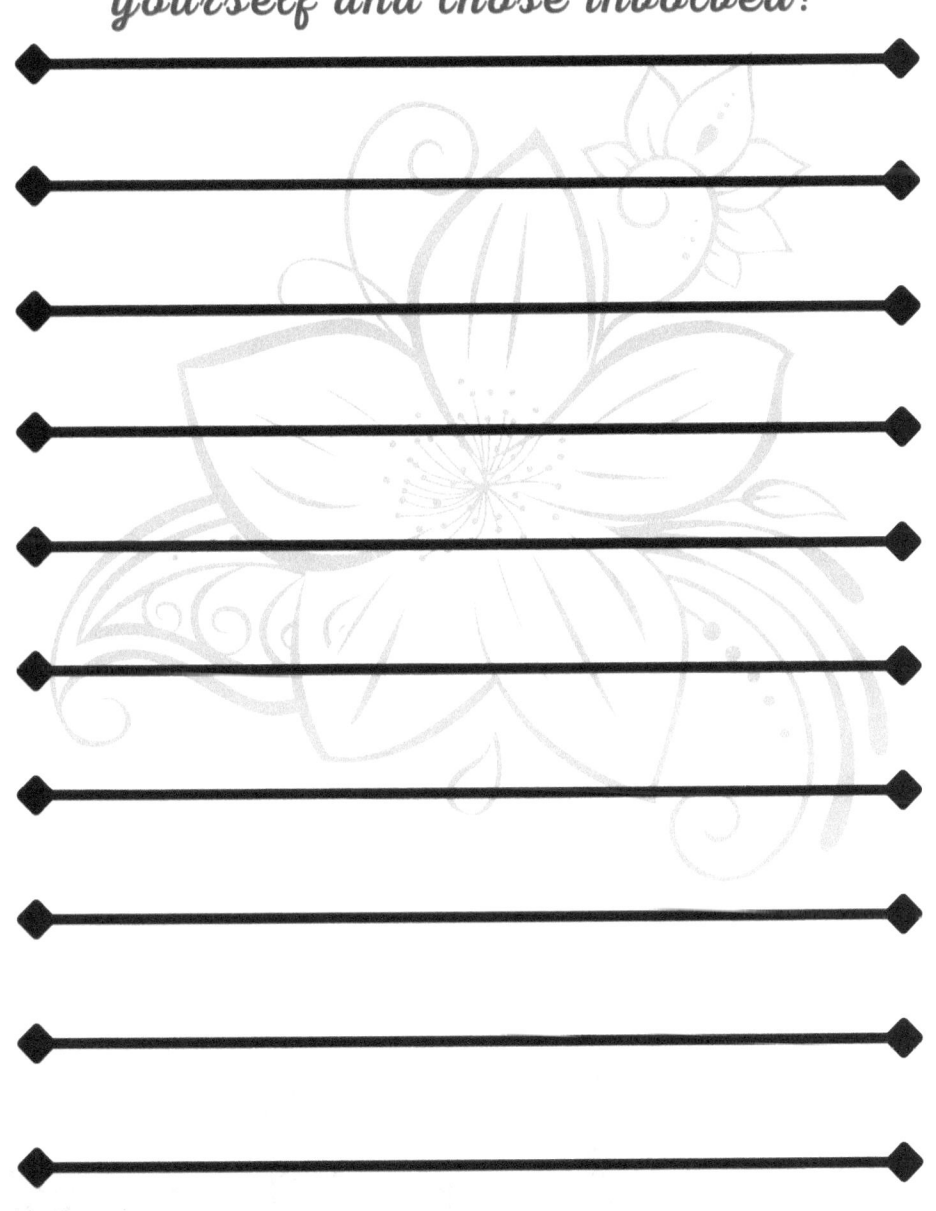

Have you ever been bullied
before?
What did it teach you?
What did you learn about
yourself and those involved?

How can you invite in more love, fun, safety and ease?

I believe in the benefits of gratitude, reflecting, journaling, sharing your story, being positive, and following your heart.
If you google or research, you can find real facts about the benefits of gratitude.
As it boosts the immune system, it helps contribute to the overall sense of well-being.
I know from my experiences what it does for me and I am loving learning as an adult that there are real scientific facts behind so many practices and values I have.

I grew up hearing the saying "stress is a killer." It wasn't until I was an adult that started to learn the truth of that. I had to re-learn and teach myself I could live differently to live different results.
I used to think stress was just a part of life and that there was no escaping it. That we just had to deal with it, embrace it and accept it. I think that thought served me in some ways. I also believe I shifted in my choices. I decided to think of the thought of stress being optional. That I didn't have to lean into the stress during difficult times.

That I could choose to think and respond differently.
This doesn't mean that I'm not human and that I'm perfect.

I have many moments where I "lose myself." I have moments when I react instead of respond. I have moments I'm not proud of. I started learning about what stress does to the mind and body, and what anxiety and depression look and feel like.

I started to learn about health in new ways and the life I wanted to live for my kids. Yes, living for others helped me live for me. We all have to start somewhere. True. But what I learned to be true is that we all are constantly beginning again. We never really start over or brand new. We just continue growing into ourselves.

Look around you right now.
What are you thankful for?
(It could be what you see,
smell, feel, hear, think,
taste.)

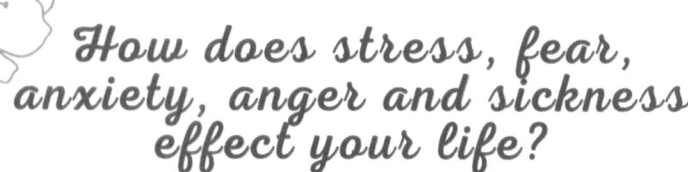

How does stress, fear, anxiety, anger and sickness effect your life?

You guys look like rich people. You are doing what rich people do"
We were told as we were holding hands walking home.
Surprised, we laughed and didn't understand.
"You remind me of when your uncle and aunt used to always walk on park street on their dates."
We laughed some more. I paused in gratitude and remembrance - I used to hope and dream for a day(s) like this.

Here I was living it and didn't even notice until someone else pointed it out.
Part of me felt guilt, that this person wasn't feeling like he has the same access to such reality and possibility.
I said, "well, he's (my husband) taking a mental health day and I included a date-time for just us two, to try a new restaurant."

He said, "yea, that's rich people stuff."
And I said, "I will take that as a compliment."
Because it is.

I have worked for several years on trying to help my husband understand that he is deserving and can have a day like today.

A mental health day.
He works so very hard, all the time.
This is what sick days and vacation days are for.
I worked even more years than that, helping myself own this new story and realization when it comes to working.

"Burn out is not a badge of honor"
Was the food too expensive? Yep, but it was delicious. The staff was so nice. And we deserve time to us and money on just us that had nothing to do with rent, bills or kids, or home.
Does he make so much money that we can just afford times like this?

Not always. Most times it's paycheck to paycheck. But we are thankful for the support, connections, community, and newfound development (mentally.)

.

It was weird, going out at 4 pm. The baby was asleep and he wants to come home for football in a bit. So, we tried something new (I even gave up the one meeting I had planned today) to make this plan work. Because he and we are very important to me

The concept of mental health, happiness, togetherness, this moment- was important to hold space for.
Abundance is all around. Money comes and goes. Time is always happening.
Create the moments you dream of. And spread the goodness to anyone watching.

Not thinking of your wallet or money, what aspects of your life make you feel wealthy?

What was good for you during this pandemic time?

What would a mental health day look like for you? (Be detailed. How would you spend your time, with who, where would you be, what would you be doing, what would you be eating, what kind of care would you be engaging in?)

The day has been filled with so many wins.

Knowing gratitude, and feeling good can sometimes be two different things- for me.

Today the good things felt really good.

Today I decided to not worry about what I had to do, but instead- align with what matters to me and let the rest work itself out. This day has been so blessed in so many ways.

That doesn't mean it hasn't been hard or challenging. But those hard times felt less powerful and overwhelming. When I break the wins down in detail, I am thankful for so much:

I am thankful for taking a morning walk with the kids because it reminds me of why I love them schooling from home while I love being home. It reminds me how good the fresh air and warm sun make me feel.

I am thankful for courageous conversations that don't have all of the answers I would love but have enough clarity to show me the way forward.
Every day has its good and t's wins. But, today is in alignment and the good feeling is so much better, even with the fears and tiredness. I am thankful for that. I am thankful for life.
2.8.22

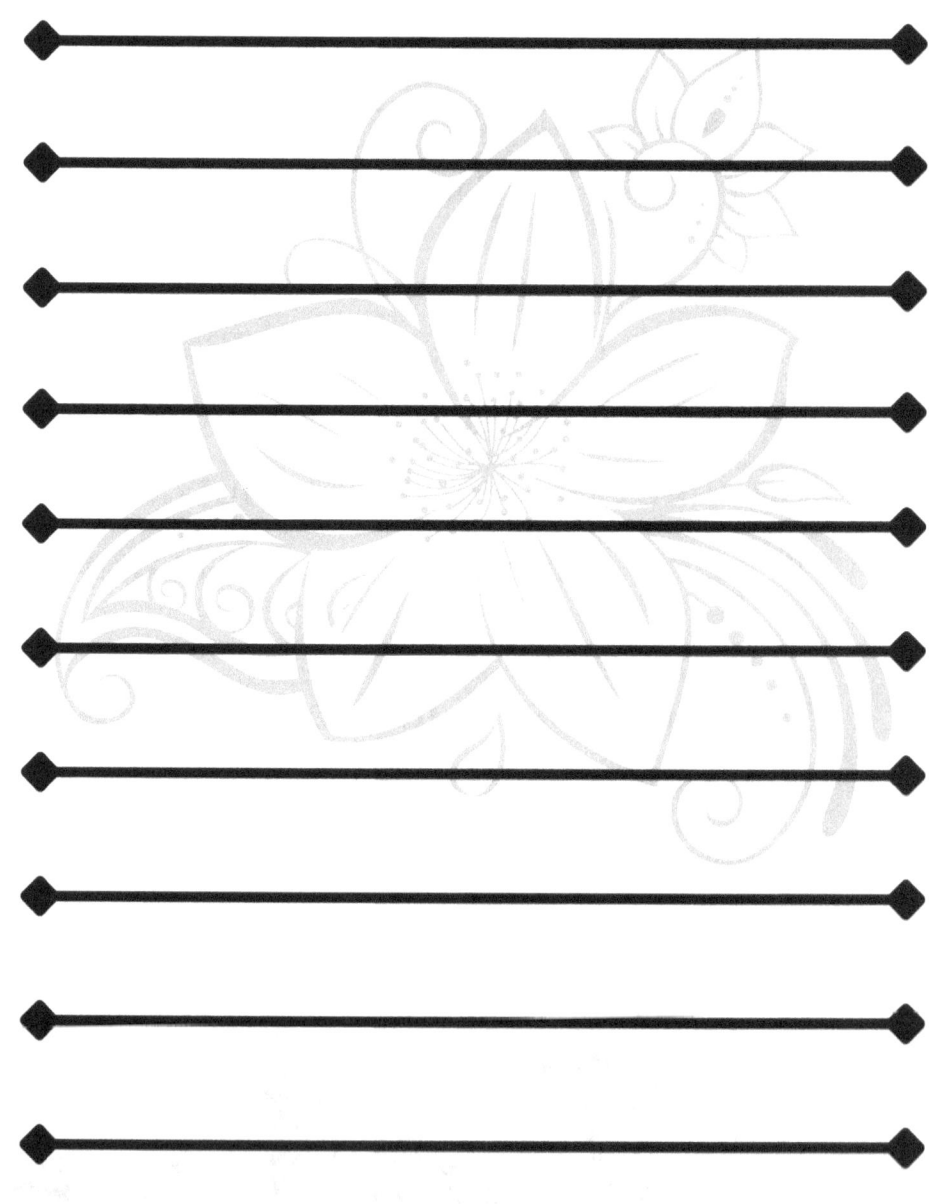

If life is what you make it.
What will you do with the rest
of yours? what will you make
of today?

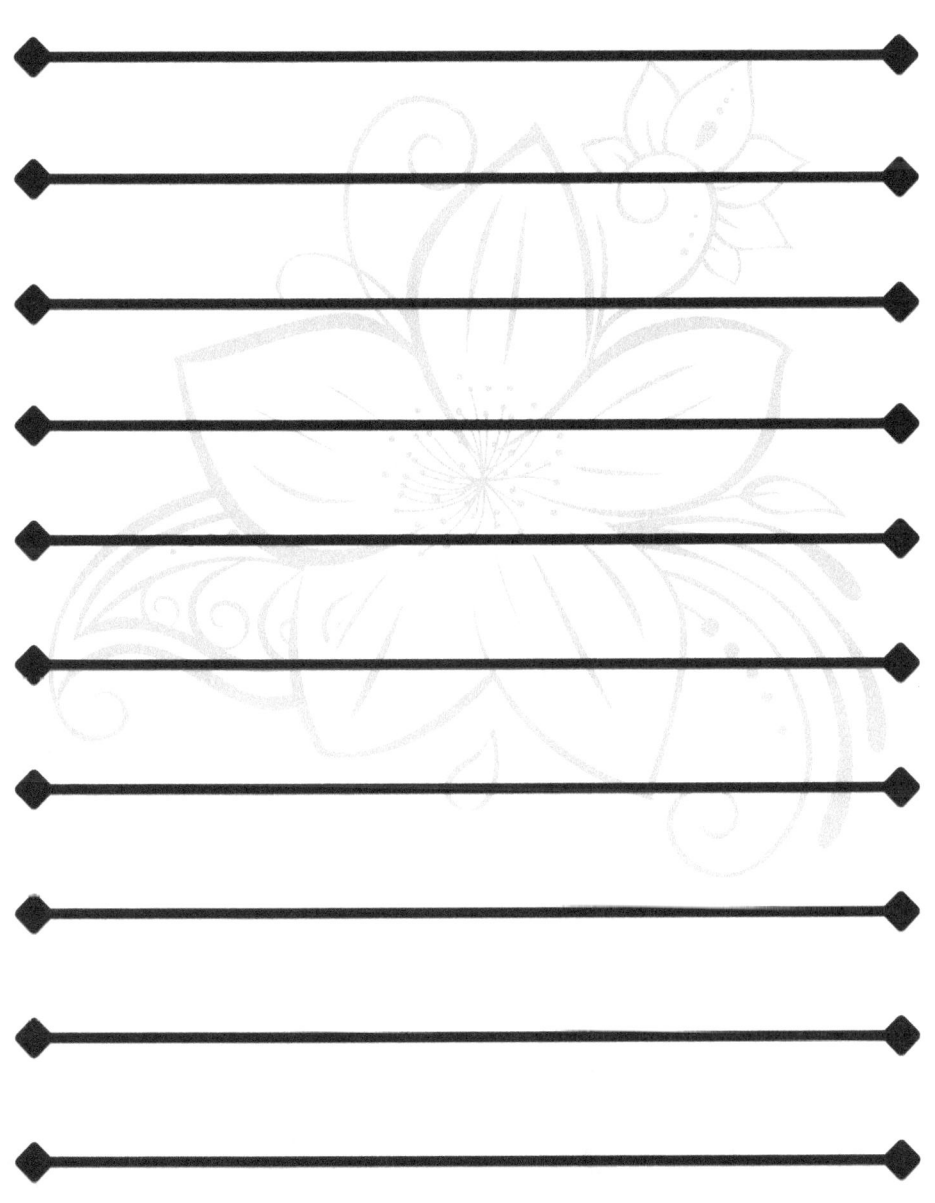

What are some of your wins?
(Today or any days.
Whatever is present and
matters to you.)

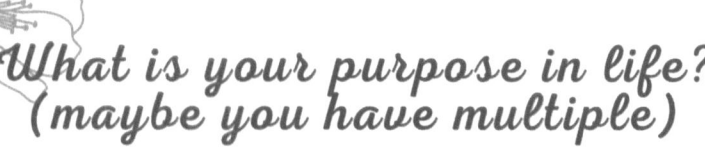

What is your purpose in life?
(maybe you have multiple)

Turn on a song you enjoy. Dance, sing, listen or do it all. Be in the moment. What about these words or actions bring you joy? What did that moment of joy give to you?

I would like to share a real experience. That many of us have experienced by this time. And if we haven't experienced it, we know someone who has or we have heard stories or seen the news.

Somehow, many of us have been affected. If you haven't, that is your journey and truth. My experience may still be of some support, hopefully in how to find gratitude.

When the pandemic was just starting and lockdowns were happening and schools closed and more, I embraced all the good I could find.

When my household got our first positive test result. When we had covid. I was able to find gratitude.

My husband was home with us, on a day off when he got a text about positive cases at work.

He found out. He was in contact with several people and would need to go get tested before being able to go back to work.
He wasn't feeling sick or anything. At this point, it was already being talked about- the roles he would be asked to take on if he was not positive and ok to work.

I went with my husband to the place he was referred to, to get tested. At this point, it only made sense he would have caught it because of all of the contact with positive cases.

At this point, I was hoping for a positive test. I felt work needed to shut down. That he and everyone needed a break. That there needed to be time off for people's mental and physical health. They hadn't had a break since this pandemic started and it was now December of 2020.

Expecting and getting a positive result felt like two very different realities. It was his first time having to take the test, which was a big deal in itself after you've heard so many horror stories about the pain .

We got the results and news.
I took a sigh of relief. That we had answers, that we knew he would be home the next 10 days, and that the workplace would close down- at least for a few days until they figured out how to manage and deep clean the space.
Of course, there are concerns and fears, and questions. How long has he had it? Did I have it? Do the kids have it? What about our kids, our baby who has had breathing problems in the past?
The year was coming to an end and we can start the new year fresh, we can build natural immunity. We can know and tell our own story and truth.

Even on week four of recovery, I started to fear we were having long-haul symptoms.

I with bumps on my fingers, and lower back pain.

Coughing still lingering in some of us. I had just ordered a kit from a doctor I had come to respect and trust. I was feeling too and never too late. I should have been prepared before sickness, but we made it through with all we had. Thankful for the pandemic support group.

I am continuing to choose peace and protect my peace. That has been what helped give me clarity and strength. And with that peace, there's gratitude. Gratitude helps me cope, heal, and make sense of life.

Gratitude helps me with anger, grief, worry, sadness, jealousy, shame, guilt, and fear. Gratitude is always there for me.

What has sickness taught you? (About your body, knowledge, support system, trust or lack of...)

What meaning can you make of your life lived so far?

What brings your soul peace?

When is the last time a day off has felt like a "day off?" How will you spend your next day off?

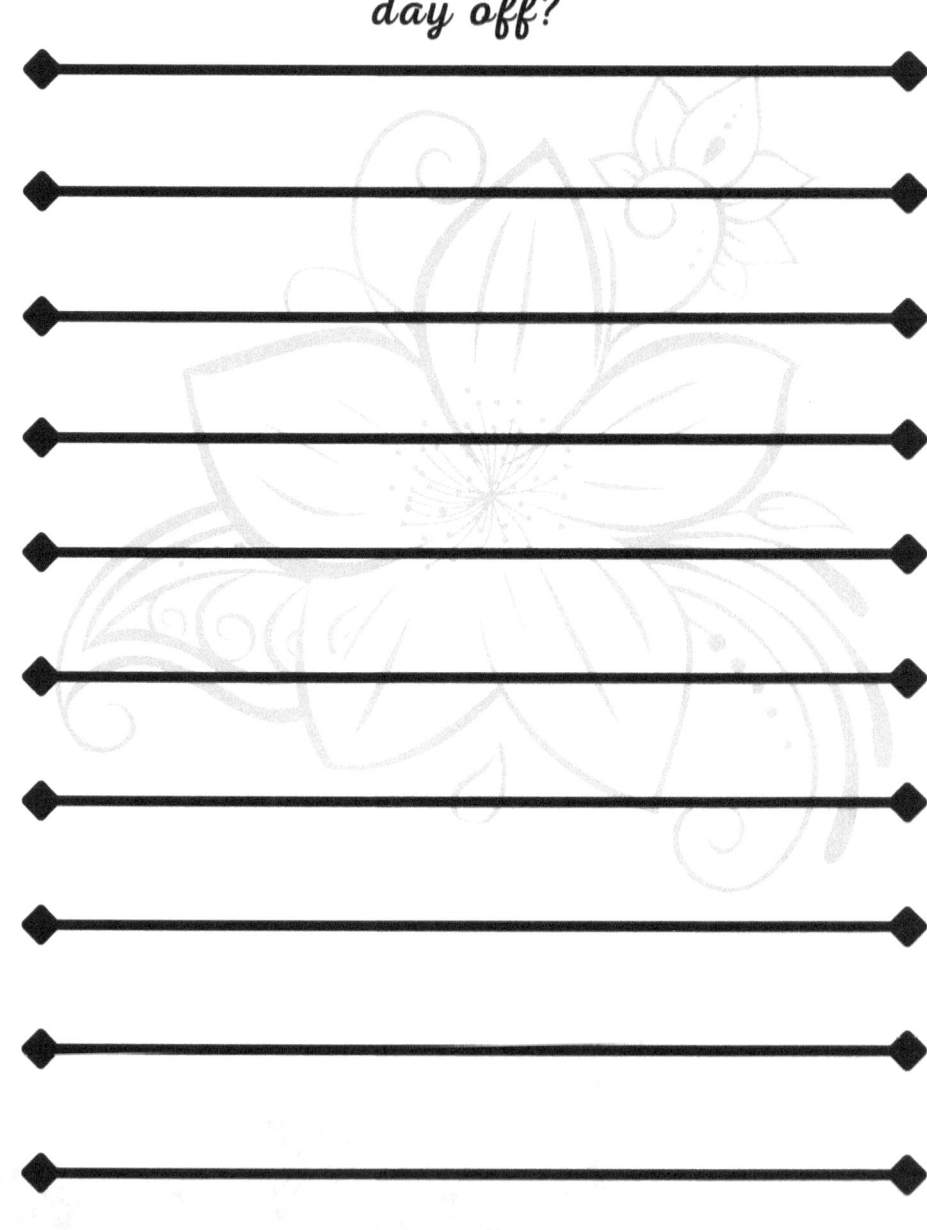

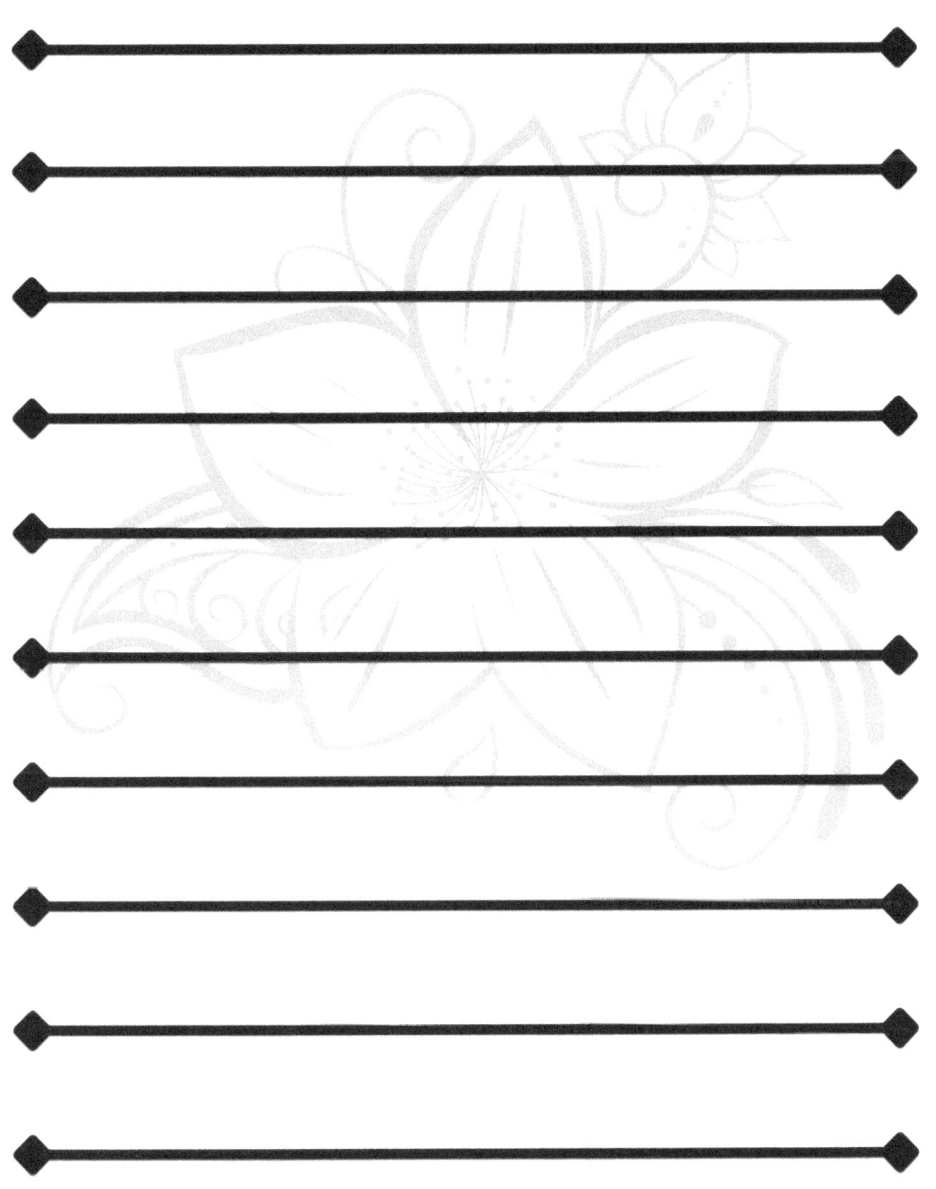

What words has someone said to you, that stuck with you?

Do I have any quotes or affirmations that help bring me to a more positive mind shift? (Write them down here as a reminder. Or, research some that resonate with you)

After a year away, we moved back to our same Alameda house in March of 2020.

I couldn't wait for music class at the library, morning walks with my uncle lu, bike riding while feeling safe as a family, walking to the movies for date night and family dates, all the restaurants on park street, joining my husband for lunch at work, my husband being able to walk to work, being around family, feeling safe, my husband going home for lunch, being closer to our oldest son, the gym, the beach, everything being in walking distance including shopping so I

could get more stuff done on my own, more job opportunities, get back to church in Oakland, support groups nearby, and have our community and friends.

For us, that was worth giving up the 6-car parking, closets and storage space in every room, 2 bathrooms, 2 storage rooms, built in house heater/fan, and the wonderful schools......

The house we would leave behind wasn't perfect although we found things, we loved about it.

It also had plumbing issues, the ants, the rodents, the distance, the fights and crime, the stolen/broken into packages, and the house issues.

No one knew during the days/weeks we moved back to Alameda, that the pandemic would happen. That we wouldn't be able to shop for storage things and we wouldn't be able to unpack still months later because stores are closed and shelter in place and losing jobs/cut hours.... no one knew that we wouldn't be able to see friends and family outside of our home for so long. No one knew so much we were looking forward to when moving back would not be possible /put on pause for who knows how long.

But even through it all, I am so thankful we are here. We have family support and feel safer. Home feels more crowded and in need of a big-time house set up but I am so thankful for all we have and dream to have.

I am so thankful that through such a hard time we landed back home. It hasn't been perfect but I have felt so different.

I am so ready to make this what I know it can and should be.
I am working on getting rid of stuff. I am working on using all we have.
I am working on making it look and feel the way that would serve us all.
It is taking time but I am thankful for the time.

Little by little, we are taking back what we once dreamed of getting back.
I am praying for life to get back to "normal" and I am excited about changes and opportunities for change/growth.
It can all still be what we make it
-6/11/2022

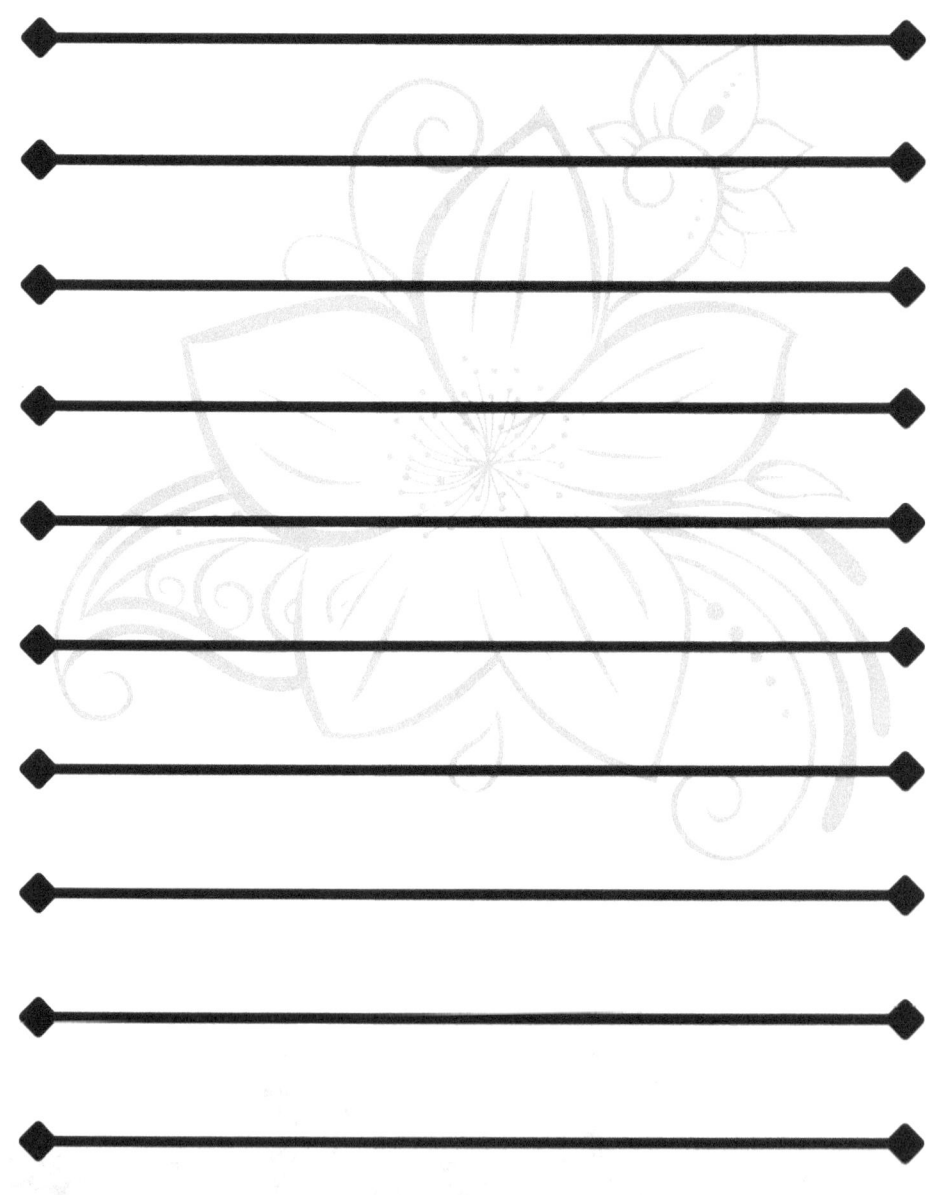

If a genie gave you 2 wishes, what would your wishes be?

(Is prayer a part of what you believe in?) If so, what are some prayers on your heart right now? (If not) What are some of your dreams, hopes, desires or wishes?

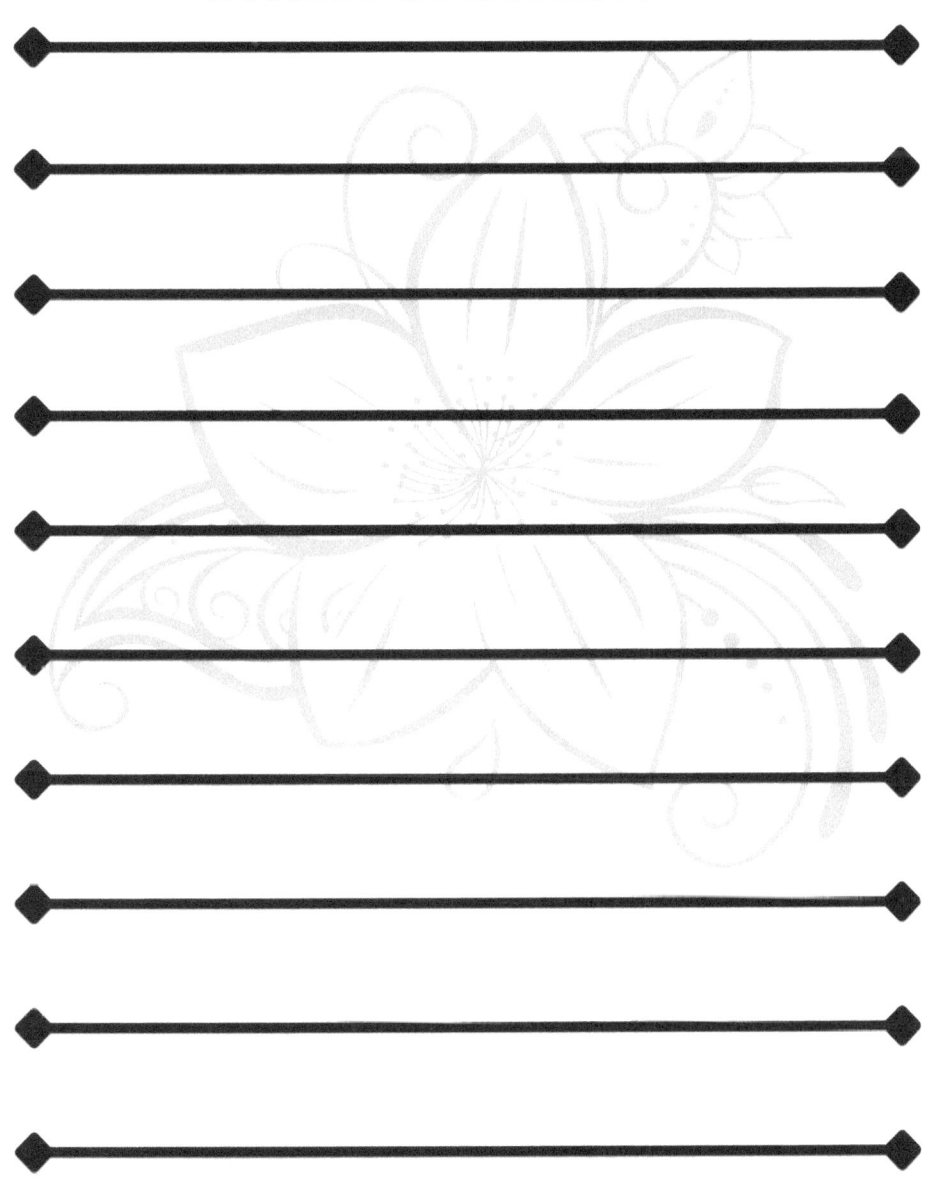

Treat yourself like someone you love. Treat yourself like something important. What self-care would you love right now?

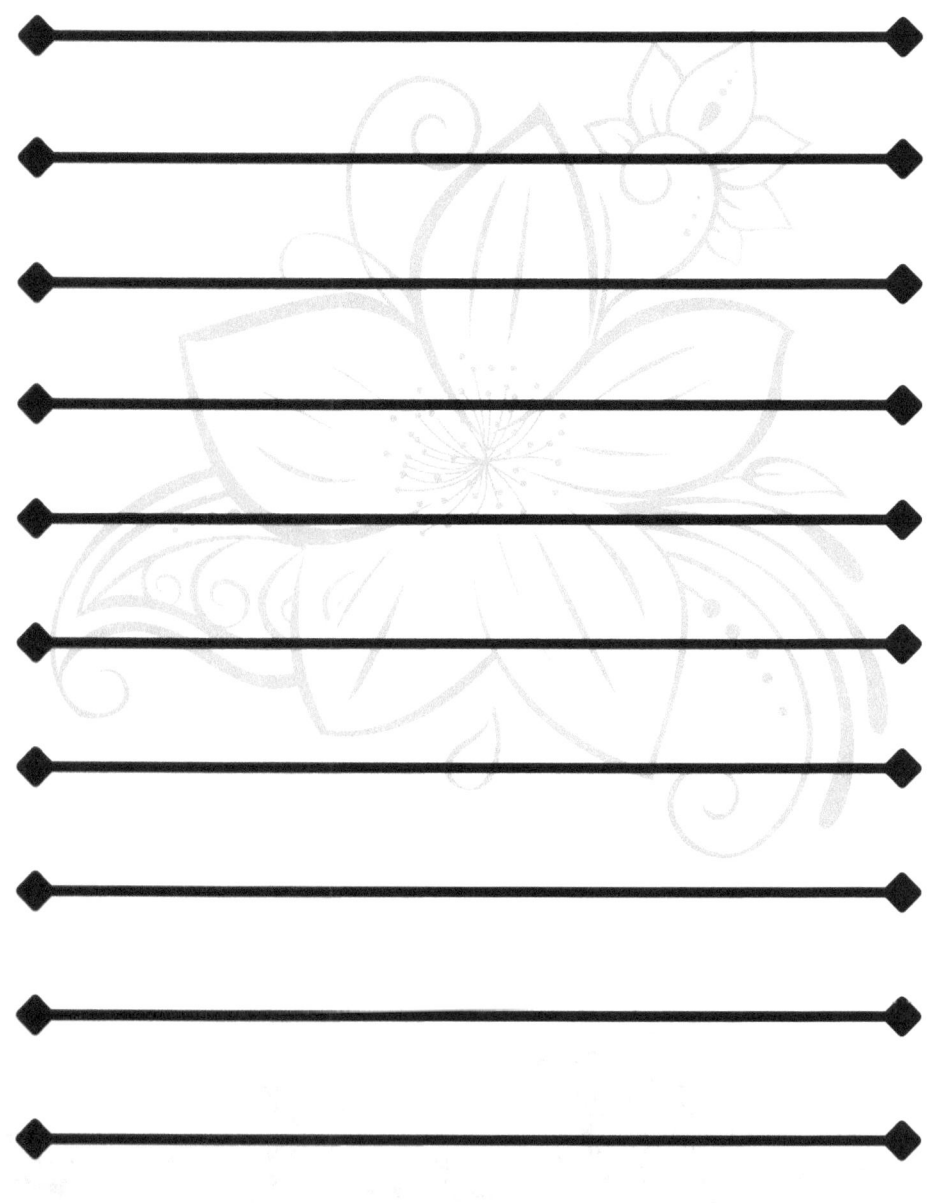

If you were your own child, or someone you love, how would you be there for them (you) right now?

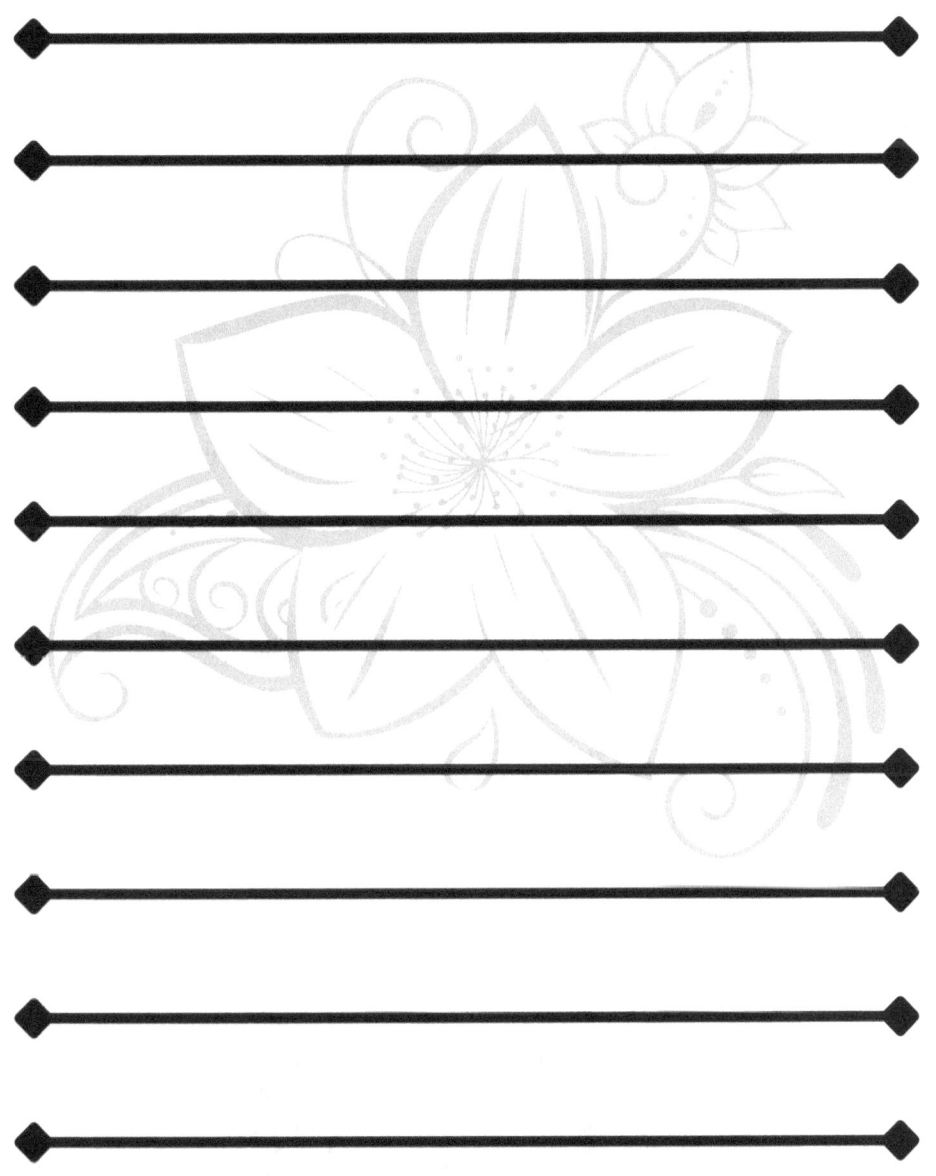

I have so much stress, struggle, worry, and pain. I feel it in my headaches, back pain, tired eyes, and body. I feel it in my anxiety and sadness and guilt and shame. I feel it in my mental, spiritual, physical, and emotional well-being. I feel it in my soul.
I have so many fears.

But then, I have gratitude. For all that has been, is, and could be. I have hope, I have alignment.
Maybe all of this stuff that is feeling "bad" is answered prayers that I do not yet understand.
Maybe it's all that I have asked for, worked for, hoped for and it's just not how I thought it might go but it may be what's needed.
Maybe I just want to be positive.

Maybe things just happen. and we find our way like we always do.
Trying to feel it all, dream again and still, accept what is, and continue thriving.

Easier said than done.
Other days are easier than others.
Some moments are harder than
others. To believe. To see.

I am trying to get clear. On my
visions. On what I would love. On
what I want to make true.
I think being so unclear and
uncertain, makes all of this so much
more difficult to grasp and roll with.
I think it's hard to find a direction to
go in when you are just going.

When are you just doing what you
"should" or "need" to, to get by?
I want to do more than just get by.

************2.4.22************

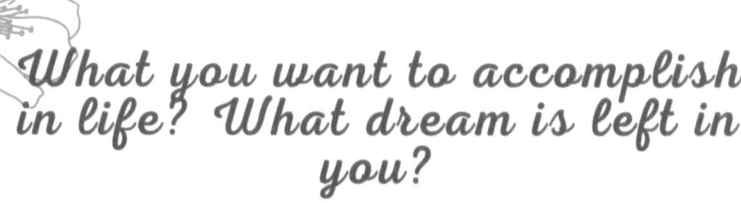

What you want to accomplish in life? What dream is left in you?

What life would I love to be living? (Be as detailed as you can allow yourself to dream)

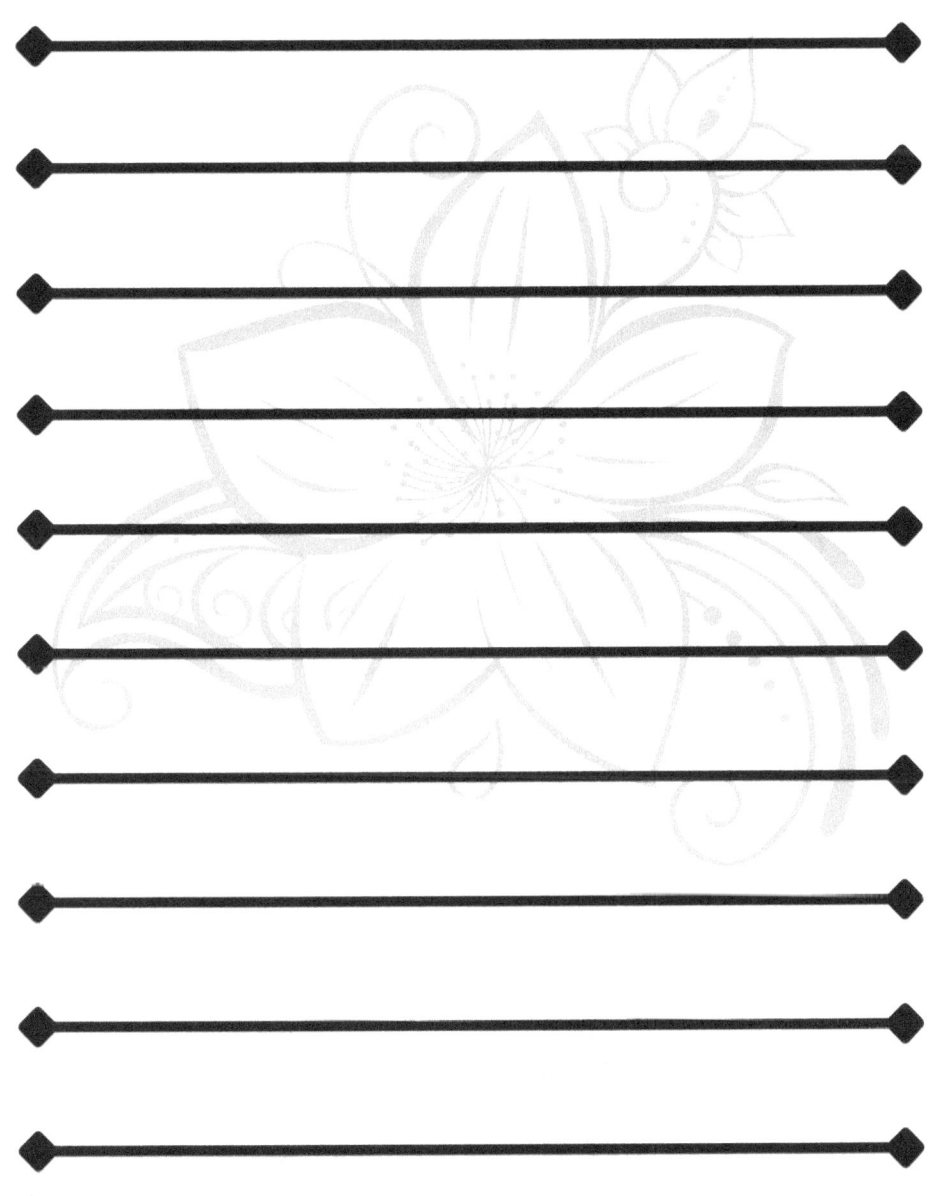

For those who are parents, parents of any kind. If you consider yourself a parent or a parent figure to anyone. We all go through a lot to become parents. Everyone with their own story, challenges, success-everyone in their journey.

For me becoming a mom was what I've always wanted. That doesn't mean it was easy. Pregnancy and birth are not a walk in the park. Through each pregnancy, I've been able to learn so much about myself. Like I am RH - and I carry something that could one day lead to leukemia.

I have learned my strength and pain tolerance and also that I don't need to tolerate all pain. I went through horrible leg cramps, head pains, and back pain. Recovering from each birth has been different. I think each pregnancy, delivery, and recovery were somehow harder than the one before.

To go through so many tests, appointments, blood draws, shots, stitches, blood clots, low iron, anemia, experiencing the scare of preeclampsia and having to be put on oxygen.

And yet our bodies were made for this and I'd do it all again. Because in the end what blessings. Then we experience parenting. One baby having the cord wrapped around his neck twice. Experiencing jaundice and meningitis. Picking child care options or staying home. Finishing/continuing school. Choosing the right doctor, school. Providing the best life, we can.

Every day I am learning and growing with each of my kids.
I have gone through so much to have each of you in my life. Physically, emotionally, mentally, spiritually.
And I'd do it all again. I loved you before you were born and I'll love you all forever even after I'm gone. (To our 4)
-----5/13/18

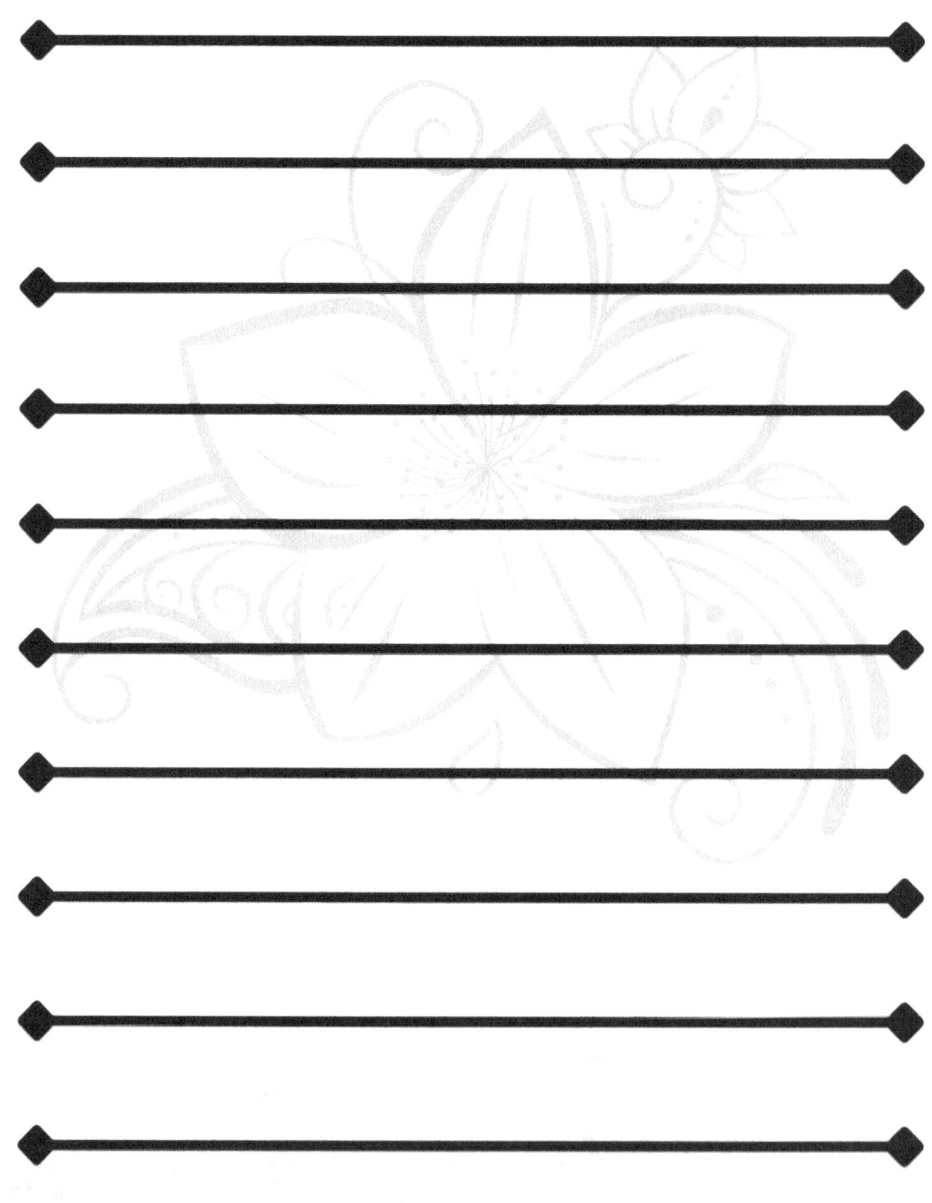

What does your parent(s)
mean to you and why you are
thankful for them.

If you are a parent, take time to write to your child or children. Write what each of them mean to you and why you are thankful for them.

How can I be of help/love, or support to this world?

How can I, someone who is struggling- be helpful?

How can I show up today?

Who am I?

What tools do I have?

What can I share?

I am "just" a former teacher

A mom

A woman

A person

A cross guard

A coach

A student

A wife

A writer

Social media connector

Virtual assistant

...... fill in the blank

And reframe it. I AM....

I AM a teacher, a mom, a woman, a crossguard, a student, a life coach, a wife, a connector, a speaker, an assistant, a believer, an author, and a person.

I AM more than any title or degree or certificate
I am
A listening ear,
A space holder
A gratitude finder
An observer
A storyteller
I am someone who's connected to others and is resourceful.
Today, - the many pieces of me. Came together to expand chalk work.
I asked questions and drew pictures- that could be for any age to engage.
I helped create play, fun, conversations, joy, thoughtfulness, safety, openness, and more.
If you are thinking you are just you and you can't save the world- even if you wish you could.
Being you and showing up as you are- is more than enough
-3.2.22

What are the pieces of me that I value?

◆————————————————————————◆

◆————————————————————————◆

◆————————————————————————◆

◆————————————————————————◆

◆————————————————————————◆

◆————————————————————————◆

◆————————————————————————◆

◆————————————————————————◆

◆————————————————————————◆

◆————————————————————————◆

Who am I?

_____

_____

_____

_____

_____

_____

_____

_____

_____

_____

How do I bring value to the world?

_____

_____

_____

_____

_____

_____

_____

_____

_____

What do I value in my daily life?

_____

_____

_____

_____

_____

_____

_____

_____

_____

_____

Seen it all a million times and yet the rules/operations/formulas aren't engraved in my brain.so much de Ja Vu but no knowledge...ugh someone please let me borrow some math DNA or brain cells! 3rd time but each teacher teaches and grades differently. so sick of taking math, failing, wasting time money, and effort:(

----6/19/12

No mental strength or physical motivation to make it to school today...just feeling so exhausted/drained and numb as if I'm in a state of shock and can't figure out what to do

4/17/12

Well regardless of whatever, I am proud of myself for going to school this whole 9months of pregnancy. I took 15units aka 5classes, last semester and got A/A/A/D/B. This semester I took 3 classes=12units and I am awaiting the grades! I'm nervous and anxious to see my grades. It was hard but I worked hard and now it's time to just wait to see when this baby decides to come

-----5/23/11

day+night classes, busy weeks/months/years/summers of taking classes I needed when they were available, 2 pregnancies, finding babysitters, catching bus and Bart, hectic schedules, classes at Merritt/Alameda/Berkeley,

Many endless hours of hw/tests, retaking classes, meetings, financial help, being away from my kids, being sad/scared/nervous/impatient...it's been a journey of 5 years of community college and I cannot wait to get my AA in child development with high honors and have my general education complete as well with honors...it's been such a long crazy road to some point of success.

I can't wait to hold my cap and gown tomorrow, it still feels like that call was a dream and this isn't happening. I'm so happy, proud, and emotional. Can't contain these feelings. And can't stop now, still 2 weeks of homework/finals/class time left to complete:)
----5/10/12

This morning I couldn't find my ring-my wedding ring. Before freaking out completely. I said it has to be here. Ever since pregnancy with my last child-my ring is sometimes too big or too tight. While cleaning and retracing my steps of the last night-I found it on the couch.

I am thankful for keeping calm for the most part. I am thankful for trusting it was going to work out. When my mind started wondering did it fall while doing dishes, did it fall in the trash, did the baby find it and put it somewhere.....as these thoughts started rushing in and emotions started to get to chaos-I found calm, and then everything worked out.

I am thankful for that.
I am thankful for day 15 of the new year. I feel like today I am pressing refresh, and restart. I have been lagging on new year goals and it is time to re-focus.
My son started this new school year at a new school in 2019 and it is a 7minute walk, depending. We vowed to never be late. We shouldn't be.

Today for the first time we looked at the clock and had 4 minutes to get to school. The usual me would race the clock, "we can do it, we have to." The usual me would start running, out of breath because we will make it. Even my son said, "let us start running, we can make it." I saw and heard him and realized what I had taught him. Both good and negative to that.

Instead, I said, "no, we can't make it and that's ok." Because we are already going to be late-we are going to take our time, not extra time but simply not rush and not race the clock.

My son mentions we can sneak in through the open side gate because we do not want a tardy slip. I say we can but we will not, we will go the way we are supposed to and we will get the slip. I wanted to teach him about honesty and what was most important. By the time we got to the school, we accepted the lady would be at the front passing out tardy slips. We check, we are 6 minutes late. The lady isn't there, we walk to the back for the morning meeting and join the crowd.

I am not sure if he will be marked tardy or not, it didn't seem like it. I stayed for the morning meeting. The kids all admired the baby and I chatted with the teacher. Tardy slip or not, we made it-we were thankful for making it at all and being safe and being ok with being off schedule.

All great lessons to learn.
I am still thinking back to someone I heard speak yesterday (Adelina) and holding some take-aways:
-we receive that which we are ready to
-welcome in your abundance
-nothing is small in the eyes of the universe and GOD! nothing is big. everything just is.
thankful for yesterday's "live." It always feels good to connect, to hear new things, to feel reassured in some things, and to meet new people. Live calls make social media feel more alive and real.

Thanks to Adelina for giving me that time.
If you start experiencing chaos today, I challenge you to find the calm and know that everything will work out how it's supposed to.
-------1/15/20

Has school ever made you feel like a failure? (As a student or parent or teacher)

What would the perfect school look like for you?

If you won the lottery, how would your life change? Would it change you?

What do you want less of in your life?

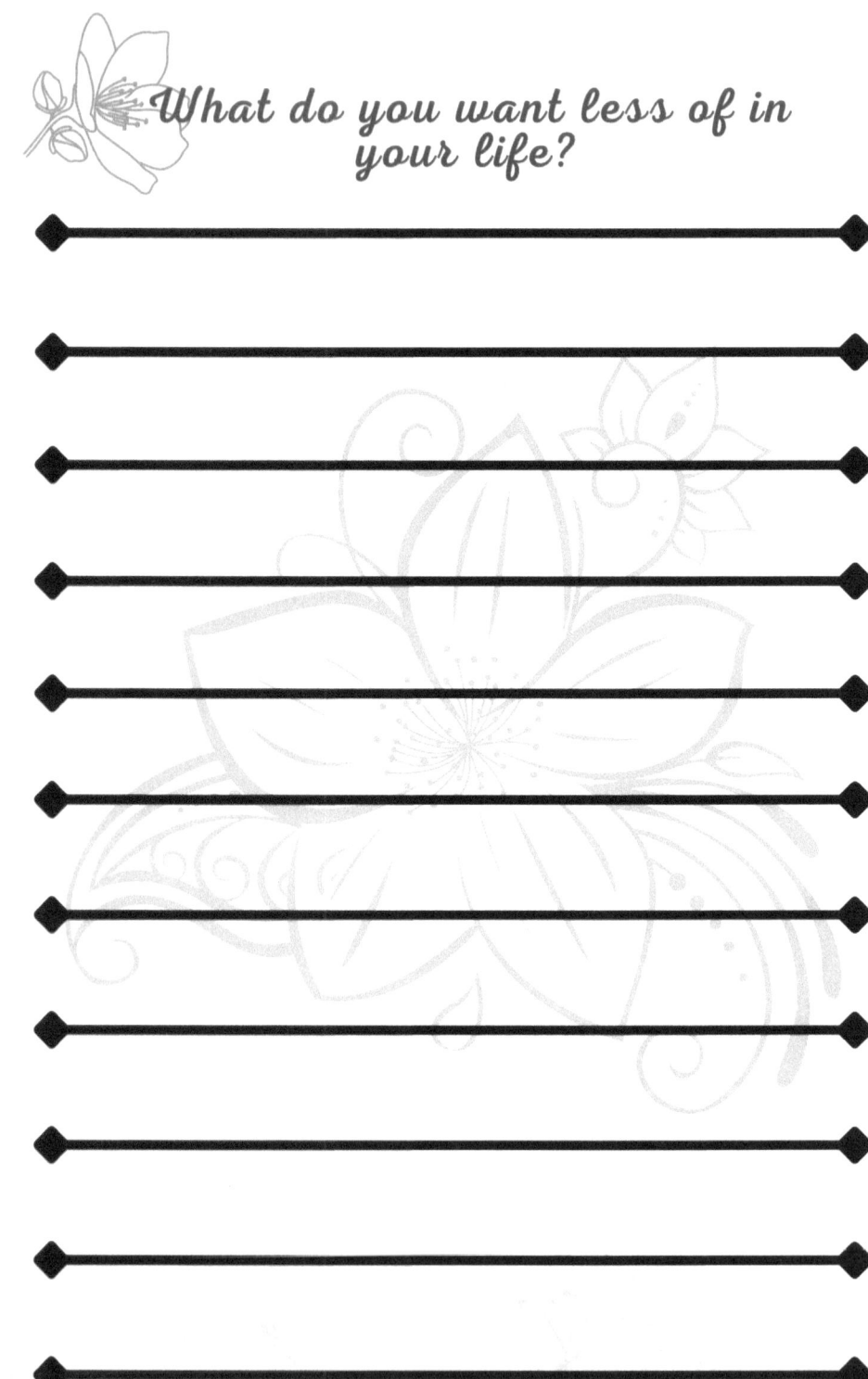

I woke up today thinking of how I "fell short" yesterday, things I loved about yesterday, ways I was able to show up for myself and others (in love and forgiveness, and ways that I still need to grow.) Today I am even more determined because it's been clear. But, I am more motivated to go to bed tonight feeling different.

That means I have some things I must get done today (which include making workout and yoga a priority. along with getting me and the kids outside/dog included. letting things go. cleaning home. making appointments. calling about this possible cross guard job.) I have some goals. I have some things to make true.
And, I need to surrender.

because carrying all this weight of wonder, fear, scarcity, being scared of the unknowns and some knowns- is not helping me. I felt them yesterday, and I feel them today. But, today. I want to just focus on the moments, the next "best" steps, and hopefully the path ahead will work itself out, however, GOD intends. But right now, baby steps.
Today will be today. Time to get back to life. get back to dreams. get back to action.
2.3.22

Have you ever felt grateful but unhappy?
At the same time.
Can you be both?
I know that both have been true for me at times in life.

So many come to me to help them find gratitude and positivity.
I will admit, that I am good at this. I kind of always have been.
Sometimes I think "Why do I have to be so positive, just let me be angry/sad...insert feeling."

Sometimes I think "I am grateful but that doesn't mean I am happy"- does that make me ungrateful? Gratitude brings happiness, so Why am I not fully happy all the time?
Sometimes I am so grateful for gratitude and I don't always understand myself.
----2/17/22

What does gratitude feel like? Maybe it is hard to answer the question "what are you thankful/grateful for?" Maybe you can think of it from a point of "what does it feel like?" example: did someone make you happy today? Did someone make you smile? Maybe that's something you are grateful for because of how it made you feel.

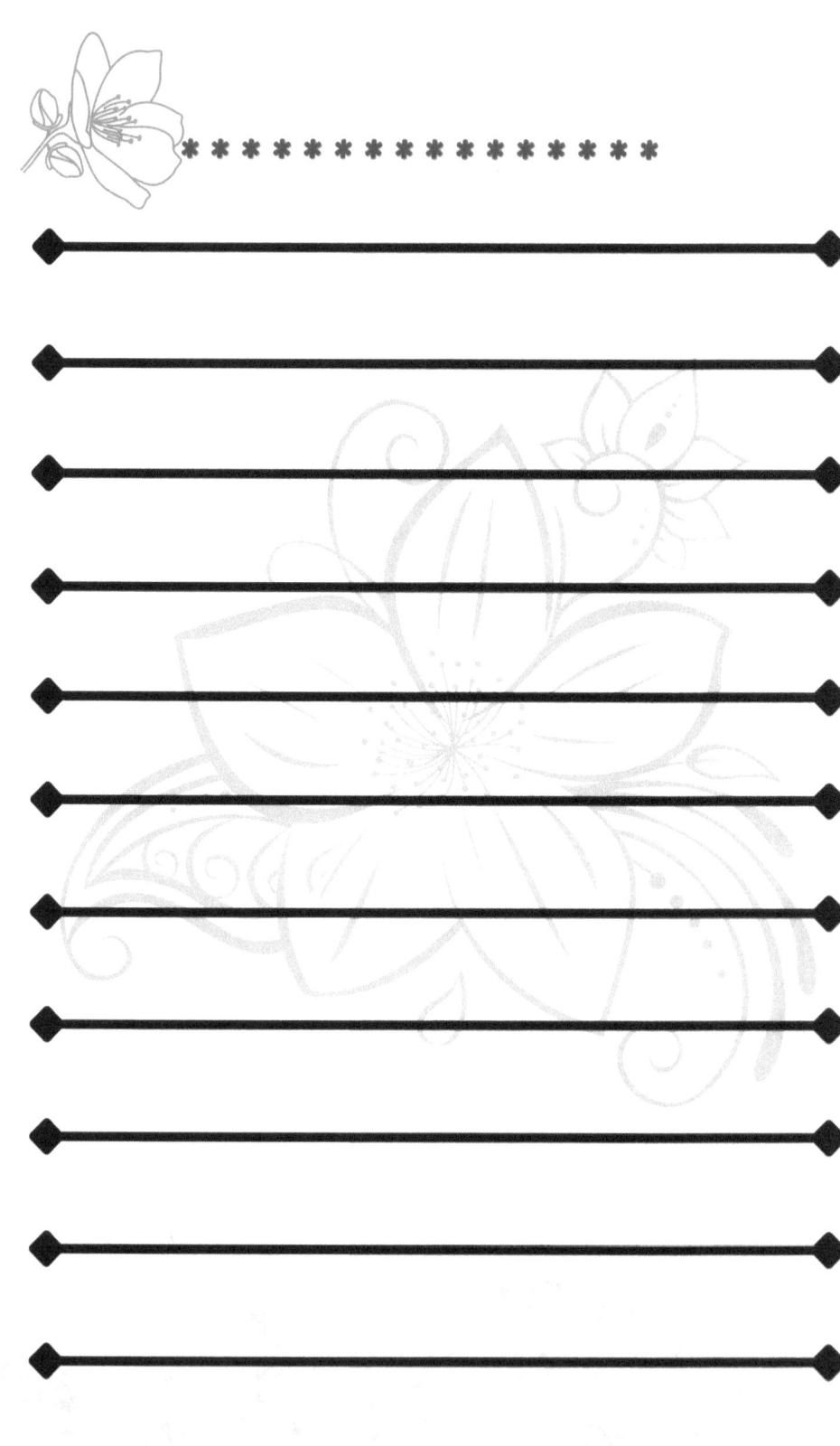

* * * * * * * * * * * * * * * *

Have you ever given someone a gift? A present for a holiday or birthday, or just because? When you are choosing a present for someone, what are you thinking of? Is it coming from a place of gratitude for that person? Most likely it is. Maybe you are reflecting on what this person means to you or has meant to you in your past. Maybe gratitude comes from there.

* * * * * * * * * * * * * * * *

I want to cry, scream and pray.
My 3-year-old just licked all over a
restaurant window!
The pre-school teacher in me, mom in
me-all of me....is thinking and feeling
so many things.

Teacher me knows she was
pretending to be a dog, knows she was
seeking her sibling's attention, teacher
in me knows about building immunity
even if this is not the way we wish.

Mom in me knows these things as well,
mom in me is upset I didn't teach her
better, the mom in me wants to
discipline appropriately while
breaking how I was taught discipline
growing up, and the mom in me wants
everyone to feel my anger and fear.
The human in me is dealing with it all,
processing and moving forward.

- I was paying for food when I hear my youngest son run in to tell me what was going on. (He was outside while she was inside with me)
My eyes see what's happening. I raise my voice to get her attention to stop what she's doing.

the two older kids outside recording, laughing and yelling...
*I am thankful I am here, in this place of dining because it helped me keep my cool. To respond and react with intention. With more mindfulness than what it could have been. (I mean if she licked the window at home,
Would we be in this position? would I be as scared or upset? would I react less mindfully? I don't know, maybe. It would be different. and then I wouldn't be here, sharing this experience.)

*I bend down to my toddler and tell her why we don't lick windows because it's not clean for us and others. I let her know I am upset. I need her to know I am upset and it wasn't ok to do because I don't want her to get sick.

I ask for water, at this point, I can't ask her to spit (I want her to spit it all out. but let's be real, she already swallowed all that gross spit, several times by now.
And spitting spreads more germs.) but maybe she can get some healing from this lemon water. so, I ask for a cup to give her water. I have her drink up. I am thinking out loud about what can she eat at home to help fight off possible sickness and build immunity.

I question myself why I don't think this way more often, knowing healthy eating is important always.
I am feeling all of my feelings
Thankful for the walk home, to continue to gather me.
I ask myself Why am I angry?
-because the older kids just watched, recorded, and laughed. They are older and know this isn't ok, they wanted her to get in trouble. but they didn't act fast enough to help protect her and teach her better (is this their job and role? yes and no. I get they are kids too, they are learning. so just like the toddler, I will give them all honesty and grace.)
-because we are in a pandemic (I don't want her doing this whether it's a pandemic or not but yes, a pandemic brings scarier thoughts)
-because it's gross (can you imagine the hands and spit and whatever else has touched that window. even if the shop has only been open a couple of hours, even if they did clean their windows. can you imagine the cleaning products used?)

Parenting, my teaching skills, my humanness.

-because of fear. fear of getting sick (because of all we are taught and what we know to be true about germs)

*I ask myself why did I bring them in the first place?

they could have stayed home, and usually when I am in a rush or want something done quickly. I do go by myself.

but...

-I wanted them to walk, get fresh air, get more movement

-I wanted the dog to get another walk

-I didn't want to walk alone

-we wanted to get my husband the lunch he wanted and eat with him and I wanted them to be a part of that

-I wanted to know they are all safe, with me

*I sure hope those inside windows were cleaned, I hope they clean them now that this took place.

Trying not to let my mind tell me all the grossness that could be on those inside windows. Mind management is easier said than done.

*We got home to brush our teeth and tongue. eat. and soon take a nap. because to me- that is healing. It's not punishment. It's what feels needed.

*I had to take time to sort out all of my thoughts and emotions and separate that from the other people "involved".

I am in charge of myself and my choices

I am in charge of me only

I am in charge of teaching my children.

So many lessons to be learned here

I am working so much on my mind shifts, language shifts

*It is what it is

*How can we learn from this?

*How can we heal from this?

How can I find gratitude?
*How am I modeling handling my anger in front of my children?
*That video/pictures will be a teaching point.... (doesn't make it ok) grace doesn't make "wrongs right" but it creates space for acceptance, safety, and space to grow. because we are all growing. we are all always learning. and when you assume positive intent + create an open dialogue, so much can grow and go from there.
I share all this, because- I am human. And, maybe someone out there has felt this or can use some of this as support. Maybe someone out there can help me, help me with the guilt and shame and anger and whatever else.
Blessings to all. I hope you can find calm in the chaos and know it's ok to not be "perfect"- whatever that even means.
(1/14/22)

Can you think of an experience that has made you frustrated, scared even? Did you react in a way you felt ashamed for? How can you find gratitude now, even if you couldn't then? How can you find some gratitude for yourself, for others involved- or even the situation itself?

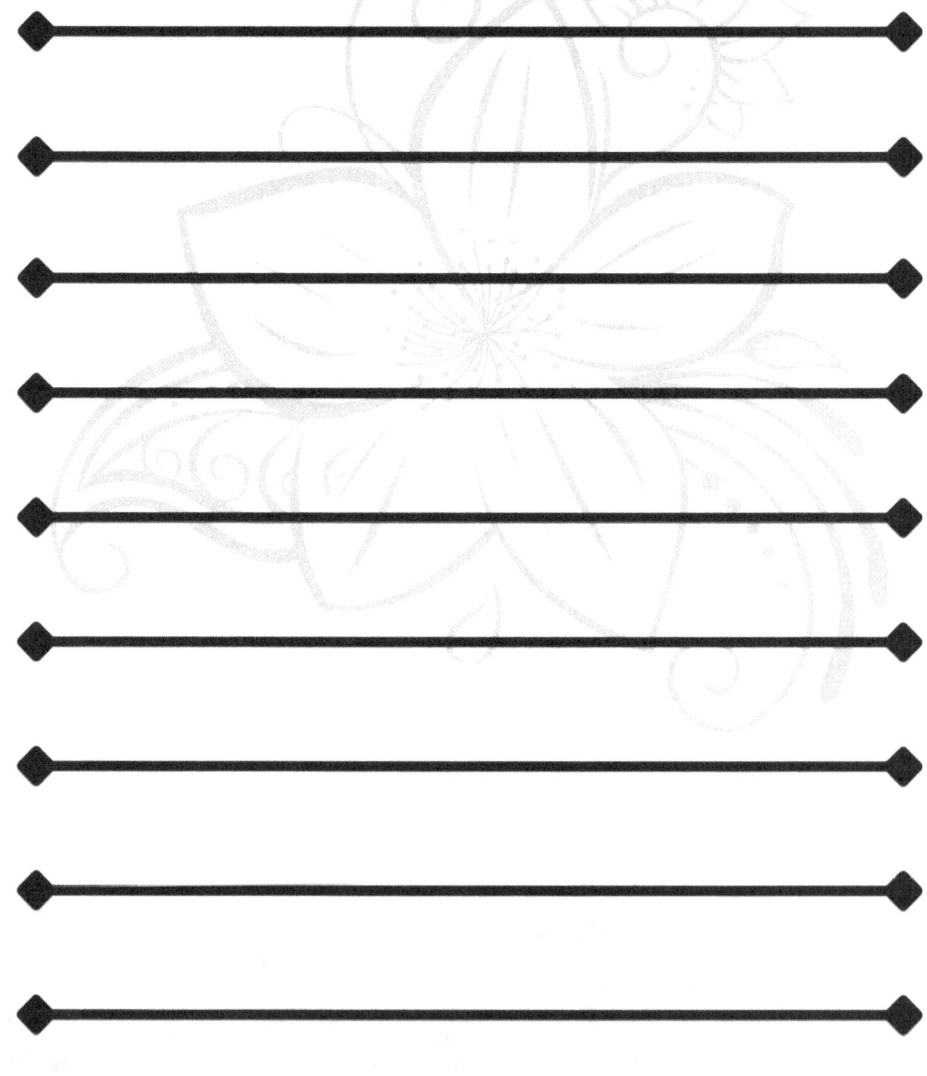

****

Let it be enough
And
Let it be good enough
- I say to myself, as I look over at the living
room that my 10-year-old cleaned.
I asked him and he did it

I am choosing to not be frustrated or
upset that it isn't how I would have
cleaned it
Frankly, I'm tired of those feelings
I shouldn't ask for help if I have certain
expectations
And also, they can't grow if we don't allow
the opportunity to take place.

Thank you, son. For listening and helping.
I only asked once and it was done.
I'm not going to redo what he's done.
I am simply going to be thankful and let it
be enough. Because it is more than
enough and more than good enough
-----1/16/22

I believe like the rain and sun have to come together to form a rainbow, that we are human and that life is so much better when you can embrace the beauty and the struggles. For me, indeed, those things often go hand in hand (the rain and the sun) you don't have one without the other

. Life is all about how you look at it. What you make of it. We are indeed in charge of our choices. We can be in charge of creating new thoughts which lead to creating new actions. We can live happier and healthier life. Stress is damaging but we can choose differently. I believe so much in gratitude.

I am learning as an adult, the benefits of gratitude and living abundantly. I have always known these things to be true but now I have different education, experiences, and knowledge to further support me so I can help others.

What can I allow to be "good enough" right now in my life?

I am proud of...

How do you grieve? It doesn't have to mean grieving only with death. It can mean grief of any kind (like moving, a breakup, something you love breaking or being lost or stolen. It can be a dream that hasn't come true or one that ended.

It can be anything that is true for you. (some examples of how I deal with grief are: I pray, go to the cemetery, talk to others, journal, eat foods that make me happy, look at pictures, listen to music, cry....) There is no wrong answer.

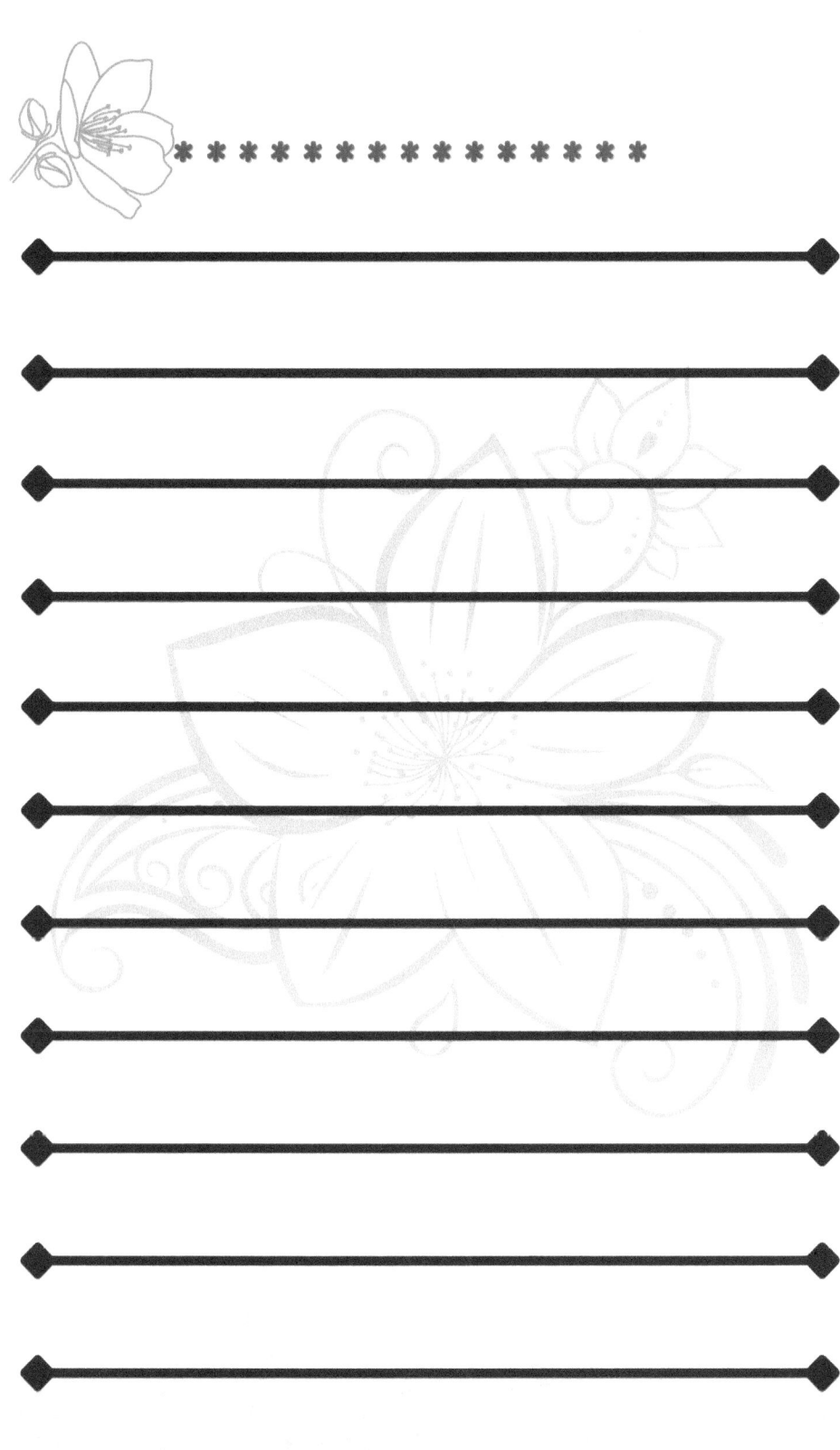

* * * * * * * * * * * * * * *

I like to end my days by reflecting on my daily gratitudes before bed. I feel it's only right to end this journal, with some thank yous.

Thank you, for supporting my author's journey by having this journal in your hands.
Thank you for taking the time to read or write, or participate in both.
Thank you for taking the time to reflect, dig deeper, process, and share this space with me.
I hope you remember that you can restart any time and as many times as you feel the desire to.

As I said in my book (Pandemic poetry and reflections) Gratitude always helps me. It helps me know life is always great and helps me see through the struggle differently.

Gratitude through my body feels necessary for me. It feels like more calm, more peace, literally.

10 distant memories you are grateful for (12/19/19)

1. Walking on my grandpa Robert's back as a child
2. Sitting in the camper shell as a child
3. Attending poetry slams
4. AA meetings with my dad
5. Graduating ,AA in child development
6. Marrying my husband-twice
7. Camping in Big Sur as a child
8. Visiting Hawaii with my husband
. Cleaning with my mom as a child listening to oldies
Rollerblading with my brother Rico holding on to the
back of ice cream trucks as a child

u can express gratitude not only for the beauty in your
but for the challenges as well. Everything is a teacher.

Disclaimer!

I am not a doctor or therapist or anything. I am just a person sharing my stories, journey, truth, and experiences. I am not telling you what to do or believe. I am not saying what you should or shouldn't do.

I do not believe what works for one person, works for all. We are all different. My goal with this journal is to share pieces of my life that have helped me come to know gratitude and the positive impact gratitude has had on me and my life.

If you leave with anything I hope you were able to dig deeper, reflect, be true to yourself and invite in gratitude.